The Physician's Guide to Personal Finance
The review book for the class you never had in medical school
Published by Two Pugs Publishing, LLC
First Printing, 2013

ISBN: 978-0-9898401-0-1
eISBN: 978-0-9898401-1-8

Cover Design by Leo at clipartillistration.com

Two Pugs Publishing
Alpha.Pug@TwoPugsPublishing.com

Why You Need To Read This Book

Few professionals will have the privilege of taking care of someone else's life. During medical school, you learned the basic didactics and skills of how to be a physician. Through your training , you learned about the many facets of becoming a doctor during your "professional" training except one: personal finance.

Of all the transitions that will occur during your professional life, few mirror that of your personal finances. Most of you will start with accumulating a large debt while you are "not working" during medical school. Then you will start earning the national median income during your residency and when you graduate, you will be earning a sizable income.

Throughout your training, you were probably told "Don't worry about the debt, you will be a rich doctor soon." But when you were training to become the "rich doctor", that medical loan interest compounded and now you have a huge debt load, you are starting a new job with greater responsibilities, and most of you have your personal finances in a mess.

This is the missing review book for the class you should have had in medical school.

I built this book like an outline review book. Skip what you know, skim over what you want to review, and read the stuff you don't know. This book is meant to be started in the front and read in order, but feel free to skip around.

In Section #1, The Basics of Personal Finance, I present a very basic outline of common personal finance topics that most people should have at least heard of. This section is to make sure we are all on the same page.

In Section #2, The Residency Years, I will discuss personal finance topics related to the physician resident: the transition from medical school to residency, managing medical school loans, setting up your budget, how moonlighting fits into your personal finance, how to prepare financially for your first "real" job as a staff physician, and how to successfully transition to a staff physician.

In Section #3, The Young Staff Years, I will present the transition into being a new staff physician with a larger income, more expectations of your time and money, retirement planning, and not getting trapped in common staff physician money traps.

This has been many years in the making and I hope you enjoy the book. Please do not hesitate to give me feed back about the book at Physician.Feedback@ProFinanceGuides.com

Cheers:
Steiny

Table of Contents:

Section #1: The Basics of Personal Finance

Section #2: The Residency Years

Part Three: The Young Staff Years

Section #1: The Basics of Personal Finance

Chapter 1
Your Budget

A budget is the most powerful and cheapest skill you can use to manage your finances.

It is the easiest way to control your spending because it gives you control over your money, before emotion starts to influence your spending. You decide how you spend your money and potentially cut expenses in one category so that you can fund other categories and consequentially, you will feel like you got a raise.

Most people overlook using a budget because it seems "too easy" to make a true financial impact or it seems "too hard" to use because they have not done it before.

1. **What is a Budget?**
   a. It is a plan and collection of goals for your money.
      i. Sometimes the goals are met/exceeded (i.e. you spend less money in a given category).
      ii. Sometimes the goals are not met (i.e. you spend more money in a given category).
   b. It should be done before the money is spent.
   c. It should be used no matter the level of your income.
   d. There are two types of budgets you should use:
      i. A specific monthly budget can be set up in two ways:
         1. **A non-zero based budget** where any left over money at the end of the month is put into savings, spending or debt repayment.
         2. **A zero based budget** where there is no left over money at the end of the month.
            a. Money is balanced between the different categories (savings, spending, giving or debt repayment) until the income minus expenses equals zero.
            b. Savings should not be solely reliant on left over money.
      ii. A broad annual budget
         1. It is used to plan for large annual expenses.
2. **How to Build a Zero Based Monthly Budget**
   a. Start listing all the types of income you receive each month at the top of the page.
      i. This is the amount of money you have to spend for the month.
      ii. Use **Net Income** (the amount of money you have to spend) instead of **Gross Income** (the total amount of money you are paid before taxes, insurance, etc is taken out).

b. Write your expense categories down the page.
    i. Start with the most important to the least important expenses.
        1. Ex: Housing, then Food, then Utilities, then Savings, etc.
            a. These categories are up to you.
        2. Be sure to have a "fun money" category.
            a. This is money that you can spend on whatever you want.
            b. It gives you some stress free money to buy that expensive coffee you hold so dear. (That's what I use mine for.)
            c. It also gives you a little bit of buffer on the months that you have some categories that are more expensive than others.
c. If there is still money left over at the end of your list of expenses, readjust the money in each category until the amount at the bottom of the page is zero.
d. Readjust the categories throughout the month as some of the expenses may change, like your electric/gas bills which fluctuate month to month.
e. Find areas where you can save money.
    i. Track your spending for a month and see where the money goes.
        1. Usually people are not paying attention and spend much more than they think.
        2. My wife and I were spending $600 on eating out during residency before we started budgeting, because we were not aware of our spending habits.
    ii. The Big Expenses:
        1. If you are looking to save some big money, look at one of the three most expensive categories:
            a. Housing
            b. Utilities
            c. Transportation
        2. The part of the country in which you live can influence these categories greatly.

Cost of Living			
	Rent	Utilities	Transportation
Dallas, TX	$950.00	$255.00	$100.00
Phoenix, AZ	$600.00	$200.00	$69.50
Los Angeles, CA	$1400.00	$126.24	$70.00
New York, NY	$2500.00	$120.00	$104.00

      iii. The small expenses do add up, however.
1. Do you really need:
   a. A land line telephone with caller ID and long distance when you have a cell phone?
   b. To drink a fancy coffee every morning when you can brew your own?
   c. To buy lunch at the cafeteria when you can bring your own lunch from home?

f. Caveats of the Monthly Budget.
      i. Realize that during the first several months, your budget will not work perfectly. . . . keep at it.
      ii. Your budget is meant as a guide, not a document set in stone.
1. Readjust as necessary to use all the money in the paycheck . . . if money is left over, then put it towards debt or savings.
2. If an unexpected expense occurs, then readjust your budget.
      iii. Put charity and savings at the top of the budget if these are a priority for you, or they will never get done.

g. Budget Busters:
      i. Food
1. Eating out
   a. This is a huge expense that can add up quickly.
   b. Learn to cook.
   c. Learn how to grocery shop for easy meals.
2. Grocery bills
   a. Don't shop when you are hungry.
   b. Shop with a list and stick to it.
   c. Consider buying store brands to save money.
   d. Use coupons smartly.
      i. Don't use coupons for the sake of using coupons.
      ii. Use coupons for products that you already buy.
   e. Shopping at whole sale clubs can mean big savings, or big spending.
      i. Cost compare prices at your regular grocery store before buying from the club.
      ii. Figure in the cost of a membership at the club for your grocery bill.
      iii. These are good for bulk purchases: ground coffee, rice, toilet paper, Kleenex etc.
      iv. It is very easy to buy a lot more than you plan when you shop at these stores.

h. Medications
   i. Check with the company that makes your medication to see if they provide financial assistance to buy their medication . . . some offer coupons.

3. **Using a Zero Based Budget.**
   a. Zero Based Budget Example: Bob made his first budget at the left, but then he had car problems which required a mechanic. The cost was $100. Instead of putting it on credit, he cash-flowed it to pay the bill by readjusting his budget midway through the month.
      i. **Cash-flow:** Utilizing current income to pay bills without using savings or credit.

Zero Based Budget Example		
	Old Budget	New Budget with Car Repair
Income	$2,400	$2,400
Charity	240	240
Savings	50	50
Rent	900	900
Utilities	255	255
Transportation	*150*	*250*
Food	230	230
Books	100	100
Cell Phone	150	150
Clothing	*50*	*0*
Eating Out	*100*	*50*
Debt repayment	100	100
Fun Money	75	75
Total Income - Expenses	0	0

(Bob took $50 from his clothing fund and $50 from his eating out fund so that he could pay the bill and balance his budget.)

4. How to Build a Broad Annual Budget
   a. A broad based plan for expenses that occur at predictable times during the year.
   b. Serves as a reminder to include expenses that are potentially more expensive so that money can be saved up for them.
      i. Examples: Car inspection sticker, license tags, life insurance premiums, birthdays, Christmas, etc.
   c. Can be done on one sheet of paper as a reminder of expenses to come

Broad Annual Budget Example	
January	
February	
March	Car State Inspection due ($35)
April	
May	Car License Tags ($70)
June	
July	
August	Wife's Birthday ($50)
September	
October	
November	
December	Christmas ($150)

5. Resources:
   a. Your Money or Your Life: 9 Steps to Transforming your Relationship with Money Achieving Financial Independence by Vicki Robin, Joe Dominguez and Monique Tilford
   b. The Total Money Makeover by Dave Ramsay

Chapter 2
Your Emergency Fund

Once your monthly budget is built, you need to calculate your emergency fund.

1. **What is an Emergency Fund?**
    a. A savings account that is used for financial emergencies.
    b. A high interest bearing account such as a Money Market Account or an on-line savings account
    c. It is NOT mutual funds, stocks, CDs, etc. that must be sold, traded, etc.
    d. It is NOT a credit card or other form of available credit . . . an emergency is not the time to go into debt.

2. **How much should you have in an emergency fund?**
    a. Most sources will suggest savings of 3 - 6 months of expenses.
        i. This is based on your specific budget (as described in *Chapter 1*).
    b. The idea is if you lose your job, the ability to work, or have a financial emergency, the cash is there to cover your normal bills.
    c. Dave Ramsay recommends starting with $1000 when paying off debt, so that you can make headway to pay off your debt.
    d. Even starting with one month of expenses is better than no emergency fund at all.

3. **How do you start one?**
    a. Start saving for an emergency fund as a top priority on your budget.
    b. Start putting any extra money towards your emergency fund as you free up money in your budget.

Chapter 3
Insurance

Warning: Do not attempt to drive or operate heavy machinery after reading this next section. Read only the sections you absolutely need . . . trying to read this all the way through will put you to sleep. Trust me . . . I'm an anesthesiologist!

Always read the policy before buying insurance so that you know exactly what you are buying and what is covered and excluded.

1. **The Purpose of Insurance**
   a. Shift risk from you (the person buying the insurance) to the company selling the insurance
   b. Cover expenses so that you will not incur financial hardship
   c. Insurance companies provide insurance to make money.
      i. They provide insurance coverage to many people and they expect to only pay money (a benefit) to a limited number of people.
      ii. Not everyone will need the insurance benefit, but if they do, they will be covered.

2. **Basic Insurance Terminology**
   a. **Premium:** the amount of money paid to an insurance company to buy the insurance.
   b. **Benefit:** the amount of money that will be paid to the owner of the policy.
   c. **Beneficiary:** the person who will receive the benefit, as determined by the owner of the policy.
   d. **Claim:** a request from an owner of an insurance policy to receive the benefit.
   e. **Insured:** the person who is covered by the insurance policy.
   f. **Owner:** the person who owns the insurance policy.
   g. **Rider:** optional benefits that are added onto a main policy.
   h. **Underwriting:** the process of verifying and determining the amount of risk a proposed insured.
   i. **Deductible:** the amount of (out-of-pocket) money paid by the insured, before the insurance pays a benefit.
   j. **Co-Pay:** the amount of money required by the insurance company to be paid by the insured (you) to utilize the insurance service.

3. **Common Types of Insurance**
   a. **Auto Insurance.**
      i. Required by most states to operate a car
      ii. Review your current policy with your insurance company to see how to reduce your premium. For example, if you have built up an emergency fund, you may consider increasing your deductible in order to reduce your premium.

b. Health Insurance

    i. Talk with your human resources department to find out what different plans are offered at your place of employment.

c. Life Insurance

    i. Meant to help provide for your family should you die

    ii. This would also provide money for funeral expenses which, on average, cost around $7,000.

    iii. Most experts recommend purchasing 8 to 10 times your annual salary in life insurance benefits.

        1. If you don't have anyone depending on your income besides yourself, then consider buying enough life insurance to cover a funeral.

    iv. Two major types of life insurance: term and whole life.

        1. **Term Insurance** - This is "simple" life insurance that you purchase much like auto insurance.

            a. It is called "term", because you determine the length of time for your coverage - usually 5 to 20 years.

            b. You determine the amount of benefit you want your beneficiaries to receive when you die.

            c. The length of time for the policy, amount of benefit, and your health will determine your premium.

            d. If you don't die, then you will not collect any benefit at the end of the contract agreement.

        2. **Whole Life** - This is more complex, because it is a policy that includes a life insurance part, as well as an investment part.

            a. Part of your premium will pay for

                i. the life insurance

                ii. the investment

            b. It is called "whole life" because you will receive some of your money back from the the investment part of your premium if you don't die.

            c. Much like term life insurance, the term, amount of benefit, and your health will determine your premium.

        3. **Term Insurance vs. Whole Life - which one to choose?**

            a. Start with Term Life Insurance.

                i. Less expensive than Whole Life

                ii. Buy a 15 to 20 year term life insurance policy, providing 8-10 times your current salary, if you can afford it.

                iii. As your salary increases, increase your current policy, or add more policies to cover your new salary.

d. Disability Insurance
  i. What are the odds:
      1. One in four 20 year olds will become disabled at some point during their career.
      2. A 30 year-old is four times as likely to become disabled than die
      3. The average long term disability claim is > 30 months.
  ii. General Information about Disability Insurance
      1. Disability Insurance (DI) is an important part of asset protection.
      2. Your largest asset is your ability to earn an income, therefore it needs to be protected.
      3. DI is designed to replace 45% to 65% of your income, should you become disabled.
      4. Some disabilities are short term (months) and others can last years.
      5. Disabling events tend to be caused by chronic diseases such as cancer, heart disease, and injuries such as back problems.
      6. Two new definitions:
          a. **Total disability** - is the inability to work at any job.
          b. **Own occupation disability** - is the inability to do your specific type of work (i.e you could do other jobs, such as a desk job, but you couldn't work in your trained occupation).
      7. Two types of Disability Insurance Policies:
          a. **Short term disability policies** are offered to cover short term disabilities, such as an unexpected surgery, pregnancy, etc.
              i. The waiting period is short (0-30 days) and the benefit will only last for a short period of time.
          b. **Long term disability policies** are offered to cover disabilities that may or may not get better.
              i. The waiting period tends to be longer (30-90 days) and benefits can last for years to decades.
  iii. Premium and Benefit Connection
      1. If you pay the premium with pre-tax dollars, then when you are disabled, you must pay taxes on that benefit.
      2. If you pay the premium with after-tax dollars (out of pocket), then you will not pay taxes on the benefit.
  iv. Individual Disability Policies:
      1. These policies are bought by you.
      2. Because you own the policies, they can travel with you from job to job.
      3. Usually more expensive than group disability insurance (see below).

4. Most private policies require a medical history and lab testing prior to issuing the policy, because disability claims can only be for disability not related to past medical history.

5. Cost depends mainly on four things:
    a. Type of disability covered (own occupation vs. any occupation).
    b. How long you need to be disabled until the benefits starts to pay out (elimination period).
    c. Amount of benefit (how much per month you will receive).
    d. How long it will pay out in the event of a disability.

6. **Some Caveats with Individual Disability Policies**
    a. As with other insurance, the longer the elimination period, the less the premium.
    b. Consider at least a three month elimination period to get a better rate.
        i.   Keep in mind, your employer may offer short-term disability insurance that may cover your elimination period.
        ii. Also, you can use your 3 month emergency fund as your short-term disability insurance.
    c. The longer the benefit pays out, the more expensive the premium.
        i.   A policy with a benefit that pays until you are 65 years old is more expensive than one that pays a benefit for just 5 years after being disabled.
    d. Buy the individual disability policy while you are young. Once you start to have health problems, it can be costly or cost prohibited to buy in the future
    e. You might be able to increase the benefit available to you as your salary increases.

v. **Group Disability Policies:**
    1. Some employers offer employees group DI.
    2. Usually less expensive than private DI.
    3. When you leave your employment, you lose the group DI.
    4. Group policies may be limited in:
        a. Their definitions of disability.
        b. How long you receive a benefit.
        c. What is covered (own occupation or any occupation).
        d. Some policies provide own occupation coverage for a period of time, then convert to total disability coverage after 1-2 years.

vi. **Some Riders to Consider for Disability Insurance**
    1. These additions to a basic policy add cost to the insurance premium, however, they can be worth it if you need them.

    a. **Own occupation** - you are considered disabled if you can not do your own job, but can still do other work, i.e. desk job.

    b. **Non-cancelable** - you own the policy and only you can cancel it.

    c. **Guaranteed renewable** - you can continue to renew the policy every year, if you choose to do so.

    d. **Partial benefit** - if you are able to work part time, then you can receive a partial benefit for the percentage of time you are unable to work.

    e. **Cost of living increase** - this increases the benefit every year at the cost of inflation, so that you receive more benefits each year to help offset the loss of buying power with inflation.

    f. **Waiver of premiums:** if you start to collect a benefit, then you do not have to continue to pay the premiums.

    g. **Cost of benefit increase** - as your salary increases, you are able to pay a higher premium and have an increase in the amount of benefit available to you.

vii. **Social Security Disability Insurance**
1. The government safety net for disabled Americans
2. You must have worked in a job in which you paid into Social Security (SS).
3. You must not be able to work at all for one year.
4. SS doesn't pay for partially disabled or short term coverage.
5. It has the most strict definition of disability, but can be used in extreme circumstances.
6. More information at www.ssa.gov

e. **Long Term Care Insurance**
i. This is insurance which is used to provide care when you can not perform activities of daily living such as bathing, dressing, eating, etc.
ii. Typically this insurance would pay for rehabilitation in your home, an assisted living home, or nursing home.
    1. By purchasing your own long term care insurance, it gives you more options for your care.
iii. This insurance should be bought around the time you turn 60 years old.
iv. It is some of the most expensive insurance you can buy.
v. It has many of the same parts of other insurance products, such as elimination periods, duration of the care, the type of care provided (nursing home vs. your own home), etc.
vi. As with other types of insurance, the cost is based on your health and the extent of the coverage you are seeking.

f. Home Owners / Renters Insurance
- i. **Home owner's insurance** is required by most mortgage lenders when you buy a home (see below).
- ii. **Renter's insurance** is used to cover your personal belongings if you have theft or damage from fire or water (a broken pipe).
  1. Many apartment complexes will not provide coverage for your personal belongings in the event of theft or other loss of your property.
- iii. Both policies may provide an "umbrella policy" that also covers your home/apartment should someone injure themselves on your property and sue you.

g. Identity Theft Insurance:
- i. Prevents identity theft or cleans up the problems caused by identity theft.
- ii. Your social security number is everywhere, college applications, graduate school graduations, job applications, etc.
- iii. Start by doing your part:
  1. Don't give out your social security number unless required.
  2. Shred all documents that have your address, bank account numbers, etc.
  3. Try to make all of your financial documents paperless (less documents with financial information coming into the house)
  4. If you do not plan on getting a loan soon, consider putting a freeze on your Credit Report *(see Chapter 7)* so that no new accounts can be opened in your name.

Chapter 4
Your Taxes

Learn how to do your own taxes. This is a basic skill everyone should learn, even if you plan on having a professional prepare your taxes for you in the future. Learning the basics is a must so that you can understand how the taxes are calculated.

1. **Basic Tax Terms**
   a. **Gross Income:** the total amount of money you earn before taxes, insurance, and other expenses are taken out.
   b. **Net Income:** the amount of money you can spend after all the deductions are made.
   c. **Adjusted Gross Income (AGI):** your total income minus deductions that is used to determine your tax bill.
   d. **Tax Deduction:** the amount of money taken off of your income, as if you never earned it in the first place. This reduces your taxable income.
      i. **Standard Deduction:** the amount of money that reduces your tax bill, based on your demographics (single, married, number of children, etc.)
      ii. **Itemized Deduction:** instead of the standard deductions, you can calculate your own deductions, such as giving to charities, costs for school, etc. and potentially pay less in taxes.
   e. **Tax Credit:** an amount of money taken off of what you owe to taxes.
      i. Reduces the actual tax amount due.
   f. **Phase out:** some deductions and credits are limited by the amount of money you earn.
      i. The more money you earn, the less of a deduction or credit, if any, you are allowed to take.

2. **Federal Taxes**
   a. Paid by United States citizens who earn an income, even if it is earned in another country.
   b. **irs.gov** - excellent website with PDFs of every form and every publication to explain tax related issues.

3. **State Taxes**
   a. Generated by several different mechanisms.
   b. Some mechanisms include income tax and sales taxes.
   c. These taxes are considered a tax deduction from your federal income taxes.

4. **Tax Brackets**
   a. Define the percentage of your income that you pay in taxes.
   b. You don't pay the same amount of money for each dollar you earn.

i. You pay a lower percentage of taxes on the first dollars you earn and, as you earn more money, the percentage you pay on those dollars increases.

ii. See the Tax Brackets below.

2013 Federal Tax Brackets		
Marginal Tax Rate	Single	Married Filing Jointly
10%	$0 to $8,925	$0 to $17,850
15%	$8,926 to $36,250	$17,851 to $72,500
25%	$36251 to $87,850	$72,501 to $146,400
28%	$87,851 to $183,250	$146,401 to $223,050
33%	$183,251 to $398,350	$223,051 to $398,350
35%	$398,351 to $400,000	$398,351 to $450,000
39.6%	$400,001 +	$450,001 +

c. **How to Use the Federal Tax Brackets to Calculate Your Taxes**

Calculation of Federal Taxes for a Single Person earning $50,000 / year

Marginal Tax Rate	Single	Earning = $50,000
10%	$0 to $8,925	($8,925 - $0) x 0.10 = $892.50
15%	$8,926 to $36,250	($36,250-$8925) x 0.15 = $4,098.75
25%	$36,251 to $87,850	($50,000 - $36251) x 0.25 = $3,437.25
28%	$87,851 to $183,250	total tax owed = $8,428.50
33%	$183,251 to $398,350	
35%	$398,351 to $400,000	
39.6%	$400,001 +	

5. **Tax Tips**
   a. The goal of paying your taxes is to pay only the amount of money you owe.
      i. Paying more than the amount that you owe does not make you a better American.
      ii. You can reduce the amount of taxes you owe to the government by reducing your AGI so that you are in a lower tax bracket, potentially saving you significant money.
   b. Keep good records of all your donations to charity throughout the year.
      i. Anytime you donate money to a charity, get a receipt.
      ii. Keep receipts from donated clothing and house goods.
   c. Keep good records on your school loans, home mortgages, property taxes, and other expenses that are tax deductible.
   d. Using tax preparation software can help you file your taxes and find tax deductions and credits to lower your tax bill.

Chapter 5
Home Mortgages

Buying a home is perhaps the largest purchase most people will make in their lifetime.

Understanding the process is paramount to making a decision to rent or buy.

1. **Mortgage Payments Contain Multiple Expenses**
    a. Required expenses:
        i.   **Principle payment -** the amount of money that goes to paying down the loan.
        ii. **Interest payment - the** amount of money that goes to paying the interest on the loan (see amortization schedule below).
    b. Optional expenses:
        i.   **Private Mortgage Insurance (PMI)** - this is insurance (paid by you) to protect the loan company if you can not pay your loan.
            1. Usually required if you do not pay a 20% down payment
            2. It costs about 1% of the loan annually.
        ii. **Escrow account payments -** these are payments you make into an escrow account, held by the loan company. The mortgage company pays two common bills from this account:
            1. **Home owners insurance -** assures the lenders that you pay your home insurance.
            2. **Property taxes** - assures the lenders that you pay the homeowner taxes.
                a. Based off the value of the home plus the value of the land.
                b. Taxes can increase during the time you own your home.
                c. Most home owners find out in October the cost of the taxes that are due by the end of January.
                d. Search appraisal district websites to obtain an idea of property taxes in a given area.
            3. An escrow account may not be required if you have a significant down payment.

2. **Down Payment**
    a. Not always required to obtain a mortgage.
    b. If no down payment is required, then the lender will usually require:
        i.   Private mortgage insurance (PMI) to be paid
        ii. An escrow account set up.

3. **Amortization Schedule**
   a. Shows how much of your payment goes to paying the principle owed on the loan and how much goes to interest on the loan.
   b. Early in the mortgage repayment, a majority of your payment will go towards interest and very little will go towards the principle.
   c. Over time, more will go to the principal and less to the interest on the loan as the loan is paid off. *(See below for an abbreviated amortization schedule.)*

Year	Payment	Amount	Principal	Interest	Balance
0	1	$716.12	$216.12	$500.00	$149,783.88
1	12	$716.12	$224.18	$491.94	$147,358.45
5	60	$716.12	$263.01	$453.11	$135,671.27
10	120	$716.12	$321.13	$394.99	$118,175.94
20	240	$716.12	$478.76	$237.37	$70,731.59
30	360	$716.12	$713.74	$2.38	$0.00

Mortgage Example: Amortization Schedule for $150k loan at 4% fixed rate mortgage for 30 years.

4. **Common Types of Mortgages**
   a. **Fixed Rate:** the interest rate is fixed for the term of the loan.
   b. **Adjustable Rate Mortgage (ARM):** the interest is fixed for a period of time, then adjusts based on an index.
      i. 5/1 ARM: the interest rate would be fixed for 5 years, then could adjust every year thereafter.
   c. **Mortgage with a Balloon Payment:** a loan with a large payment due at the end of the loan.
   d. **Length of Payments:** most common are 15 year or 30 year mortgages.

5. **Up-Front Cost of Buying a Home**
   a. Closing costs
      i. This can be negotiated during the buying process.
   b. Down payment
      i. You get a better deal on loans if you have at least a 20% down payment.
         1. You usually don't have to pay for PMI.
         2. You are not required to carry an escrow account.

6. **Cost of Selling a Home**
   a. Typically, 6% of the selling price will go to realtors.
      i. They are paid by the sellers out of the sales price of the home.
      ii. Typically 3% goes to the selling agent and 3% to the buyer's agent
   b. You are paying to make sure all the legal paperwork is in order and your home is sold.

Chapter 6
Treating Your Debt

1. **Debt Management vs. Debt Treatment**
   a. Some people's overall plan is debt management, pay the minimal payments and let the debt work itself out.
   b. I would encourage you to treat the debt (get out of debt) . . . don't manage it.
   c. Two main strategies to pay off debt:
      i. **Interest Rate Model:** Pay minimum payments on all the loans and concentrate on paying extra money to the largest interest rate first.
      ii. **Lone Size Model:** Pay minimum payments on all the loads and concentrate on paying extra money to the debt with the smallest amount first.

2. **Interest Rate Model for Debt Repayment:**
   a. Very popular method for paying off loans
   b. **The theory**
      i. Higher interest rate loans cost more money the longer you have the loan.
      ii. You want to pay the highest interest rate loans off faster because these loans cost you the most amount of money.
   c. **The mechanics**
      i. You focus on the loan with the highest interest rate, paying extra on that loan and paying minimum payments on all the other loans.
      ii. When the highest interest rate loan is paid off, all the money that was going to it, plus the extra payments are focused on the next highest loan, and so on.
      iii. In the example below, extra money would be sent to CC #1, because it has the highest interest rate.

Common Debt Payment Plan Used - Highest % Rate First			
Type of Debt	Minimum Payment	Debt	% Rate
Credit Card #1	$25.00	$15,000	24.0
Credit Card #2	$15.00	$5,000	12.0
Bank Loan	$124.00	$10,000	8.5
Student Loan #1	$1,187.02	$100,000	7.5
Student Loan #2	$119.00	$6,000	7.0

3. **Loan Size Model - Paying off Loans Smallest to Largest:**
   a. Made popular through Dave Ramsay.
      i. He calls it "The Debt Snowball"

b. **The theory**
   i. Loans are paid off in the order of smallest loan amount to largest loan amount.
   ii. No attention is paid to the interest rates.
   iii. This arrangement allows for some "quick wins". By getting the smaller loans paid off sooner, you are motivated to pay off the other loans.

c. **The mechanics**
   i. You pay extra money to the smallest loan and make minimum payments on all the others.
   ii. This allows you to pay off the smaller loan faster, then add that money to the next loan and "snowball" the payments.
   iii. Each time you pay off a loan, the amount going to the next loan has more money going to it.
   iv. In the example below, extra money would be sent to CC #2, because it is the smallest amount.

Loan Size Model Used - Pay off the Smallest Loan First			
Type of Debt	**Minimum Payment**	**Debt**	**% Rate**
Credit Card #2	$15.00	$5,000	12.0
Student Loan #2	$119.00	$6,000	7.0
Bank Loan	$124.00	$10,000	8.5
Credit Card #1	$25.00	$15,000	24.0
Student Loan #1	$1,187.02	$100,000	7.5

4. **Which Debt Treatment Plan is Right For You?**

a. I am completely biased.
   i. My wife and I used the Loan Size Model to pay off our family's debt and we found it to be very motivational.

b. **The Ramsay rationale**
   i. While paying off the higher interest rate seems like good mathematics, there is an emotional tie to debt. Each loan you pay off will help you feel better about your finances.
   ii. When the first loan was paid off and we used the money to start working on the next loan it was motivating to keep going.
      1. It gave us the encouragement to continue working through the debt till we paid off everything but the house.

5. **Resources**

a. <u>The Total Money Makeover</u> by Dave Ramsay

Chapter 7
Your Credit Report

1. **Your Credit Report**
   a. A record of all the credit cards, loans, and mortgages that you have had in the past and present.
   b. It also has a list of all the companies that have requested your credit score.
2. **FICO Score**
   a. Named for Fair Isaac Corporation, which created the credit scores.
   b. It is a score that attempts to determine if companies should extend credit to you, based on your past handling of debt.
   c. **A Higher Credit score is considered better**
      i. The world of personal finance puts a lot of emphasis on your credit score.
         1. It is a numbers game and can affect multiple aspects of your financial life.
            a. Your score can affect your auto insurance premium.
            b. It may determine if you can qualify to rent an apartment.
            c. It determines if you can qualify for a home mortgage loan.
3. **How Your FICO score is Calculated:**
   a. Payment history (35%)
   b. Amounts owed (30%)
   c. Length of credit history (15%)
   d. New credit (10%)
   e. Types of credit used (10%)
4. **Check your Credit Report at least Annually**
   a. Your credit report is kept at three different companies:
      i. **Equifax**
      ii. **Experian**
      iii. **TransUnion**
   b. You can obtain a free credit report annually (you have to pay for your score) at www.annualcreditreport.com.
   c. Make sure that all the information on the report is accurate.
      i. If it is not accurate, then you can write a letter to have it corrected.

Chapter 8
Über Basic Introduction to Investing

Investing is using money that you have earned to make more money. Your money will work harder than you ever can . . . it can work for you 24/7, if you invest it properly.

Investing is beyond the size/scale of this book. However, below is an über basic introduction to the subject.

1. **Where to Put Your Money**
    a. **Checking Account**
        i. This is where money is first deposited from a paycheck.
        ii. Consider this account a waypoint for your money, not a destination.
    b. **Savings Account**
        i. Transfer a portion of your paycheck for:
            1. An emergency fund.
            2. Saving up for a large purchase you plan to make within five years.
    c. **Money Market Account**
        i. Tends to have a higher interest rate than savings accounts
        ii. It has limitations on the number/amount of withdraws in a month, usually 6 withdraws.
        iii. Also a good place for an emergency fund or saving for large purchases
    d. **Certificates of Deposit (CD)**
        i. Tend to have a higher interest rate than savings or money market accounts
        ii. You can purchase CDs for different periods of time.
            1. 6 month & 1,3,5, and 10 years are common
        iii. There is a penalty if the money if withdrawn before the CD matures (the length of time of the CD).
    e. **Stocks**
        i. Provides part ownership in a company
        ii. Some stocks pay a dividend, which is money given out to the shareholders based on the amount of stock you own.
            1. Dividends can be paid quarterly, semi-annually, or annually.
        iii. You only pay income taxes on this money when you sell the stock.
    f. **Mutual Funds**
        i. Collections of stocks that are bundled together based on an investment strategy
        ii. You tend to have less risk compared to individual stocks because your investment is with many companies, not just one.

    iii. Types of Mutual Funds
1. **Load funds:** require you to pay a fee upfront for investing in the fund.
2. **No load funds:** do not require you to pay an upfront fee to buy the mutual fund.
3. **Actively managed funds:** those mutual funds which buy and sell stocks based on what a fund manager thinks will provide the best increase in the value of the fund.
   a. These tend to be more expensive for fund managers to run.
      i. 1.5% - 3% cost of assets to manage
4. **Passively managed funds:** those mutual funds which buy and sell stocks within the fund based off of an index.
   a. **example:** S&P 500 index - this type of mutual fund contains the top 500 US companies' stocks.
   b. These tend to be less expensive for fund managers to run.
      i. 0.2% - 0.8% cost of assets to manage

g. **Bonds**
   i. Used by governments and private companies to raise money
   ii. You buy a bond and the government or company agrees to pay you back the money, plus interest.
   iii. These tend to be considered by some to be a safe investment.

h. **Real-estate**
   i. Land, housing, or commercial property that you own with the intent that the property will be worth more money over time.

2. **Liquid vs. Ill-liquid**
   a. **Liquid:** Accounts that hold money that can be easily accessed:
      i. checking account, savings account, or money market account
   b. **Ill-liquid:** Accounts that require something to be sold, or have a penalty associated with them if the money is taken out before a specific time.
      i. CDs, stocks and mutual funds

3. **Resources**
   a. The Boggleheads' Guide to Investing by Larimore, Lindauer, LeBoeuf and Bogle.
   b. www.whitecoatinvestor.com

Chapter 9
Saving for Higher Education

There are multiple ways to save for your child's higher education.

1. **Places to Save**
   a. **Savings Account**
      i. <u>Pro:</u> Easy to set up.
      ii. <u>Con:</u> Does not earn much interest.
         1. You pay income tax on any gains (it does not grow tax free).
   b. **Pre-Paid State Plans:**
      i. <u>Pro:</u> Pay today's tuition now, so that in the future, you don't have to pay tuition at state schools.
      ii. <u>Con:</u> State specific - you/your child can only go to your state's school.
         1. Therefore, it won't help for out of state / private schools.
   c. **529 Plans**
      i. <u>Pro:</u> Money grows tax free
         1. Money can be taken out of these accounts for higher education.
         2. Each family member can have their own account.
         3. Money can be transferred to other family member accounts.
         4. You can invest in any state's 529 and you/your child does not have to go to school in that state.
      ii. <u>Con:</u> Money is placed in plans after taxes (no reduction in your AGI when filing taxes).
         1. If you take money out of these accounts for other reasons than higher education, you will have to pay a penalty on the earnings, usually 10% on the growth of the plan.
2. **How Much to Save**
   a. Depends on multiple factors
      i. How long until your child starts higher education?
      ii. How much will it cost when the child gets there?
         a. Tuition has been increasing at a rate of 7% annually.
      iii. How much do you plan on funding your child's education.
   b. Calculate how much to save at www.savingforcollege.com.

3. **Resources**
   a. www.savingforcollege.com
      i. Allows you to calculate how much you need to save based on the amount you have already saved and how long your until children start college.
      ii. Great place to evaluate different State's 529 plans
         1. You don't have to live in a particular state to use their 529 plan.

Chapter 10
Paying for Higher Education

There are a variety of ways to pay for education.

Although it is often stated "Invest in Yourself", it doesn't mean you should overspend or go into debt to pay for an education that you won't use.

1. **Savings**
   a. Money saved by the student or the student's family for the purpose of paying for undergraduate/graduate level education.
   b. This money can be saved in a variety of accounts:
      i. a regular savings account
      ii. a 529 plan
      iii. any other type of account where money is invested

2. **Grants/Scholarships**
   a. Money paid to a student by an individual or an organization to help defray the cost of an education.
   b. Does not have to be repaid
   c. **Grants**
      i. Usually need-based
      ii. Some may require other criteria such as a minority status or a residency requirement.
   d. **Scholarships**
      i. Usually merit-based
      ii. Some may have other requirements, such as a minimum grade point average, to continue to receive the support.

3. **Work-Study Programs**
   a. Usually needs based programs set up through colleges and universities which allow students to work at the university
   b. The amount of money that can be earned by the student is limited by the amount of financial need.

4. **Part-time work**
   a. <u>Pro:</u> No restrictions on the amount of money that can be earned.
      i. It is not needs-based.
      ii. It does not require a federal application.
   b. <u>Con:</u> Time commitment: time spent working may interfere with classes and studying.

5. **Loans**
   a. Financially, the least desirable because the money must be paid back with interest
   b. Most government loans assume that you are a single person, so the amount of assistance is based off of this assumption (see full discussion below).
      i. Therefore, these are not designed to support an entire family.
   c. **Government Loans**
      i. **Subsidized loans:** interest on subsidized loans is paid by the government while you are in school, and sometimes for a longer period of time.
         1. These interest payments save a ton of money during the life of the loan.
      ii. **Unsubsidized loans:** interest starts to accumulate the moment you take out the loan.
         1. If you took out a loan for $10,000 at the start of your education, the amount you need to repay will be much higher by the time you graduate.
   d. **Private School Loans**
      i. Tend to have higher interest rates
      ii. Interest accumulates the moment the loan is taken out.
      iii. Does not tend to be as desirable as government loans
   e. **Student Financial Assistance**
      i. **Process:**
         1. Contact **your school's financial aid office** to enlist their help with the paperwork.
         2. Apply for the Free Application for Federal Student Aid (FAFSA) at www.fafsa.gov.
            i. Apply early - if there is a problem with the application, you may need to fix it before the deadline.
            ii. Some private loans also require that you fill out the FAFSA paperwork.
         3. Determine if you want to apply based on your savings and income, or if you want to include your parents in the need-based determination.
            a. Some colleges and universities require you to include your parents on the application.

ii. **The Award Letter** (*see below*)
   1. Describes the amount of financial aid you have been awarded
   2. The cost of attendance, expected family contribution, outside scholarships and the financial need are included in the letter.
      a. You accept or decline the terms of the award and reply by the deadline.
      b. Hold on to all of your paperwork, because you will have to re-apply each year for your assistance.

Sample Financial Aid Award Package - Undergraduate School		
Total Cost of Attendance	$24,000	
Expected Family Contribution		$1,623
Outside Scholarship		$2,000
Financial Need		$20,377
Federal Pell Grant		$3,900
State Scholarship Grant		$2,000
Institutional Grant		$5,000
Federal Perkins Loan		$4,000
Federal Direct Loan		$2,977
Federal Work-Study		$2,500
Total Award		$20,377

6. **Resources**
   a. Federal Student Aid Program - www.fafsa.gov
   b. www.savingforcollege.com

Chapter 11
Retirement Savings

The phenomenon of retirement is a new concept within the last 100 years. In the past, people would work until they physically couldn't work anymore, or they died. Today, many people are looking forward to retiring early. The basic idea is to invest money while you are working, let it grow, then live off the investment income when you are not able, or don't want, to work anymore.

1. **Basic Types of Plans**
   a. Company Based Plans.
   b. Personal Plans.

2. **Company Based Retirement Plans**
   a. **Basic Types of Plans**
      i. **Defined Benefit Plans**
         1. Also known as pension plans
         2. A company provides this service to you as a benefit.
         3. The benefit is defined, in that the amount of the benefit is based on
            a. The amount of time with the company
            b. The position obtained.
         4. These types of plans can not be transferred from company to company if you change jobs.
         5. These are becoming rare as companies shift the responsibility of funding retirement accounts to employees.
      ii. **Defined Contributions Plans**
         1. Most common type of retirement plan today
         2. You contribute a set amount of money from each paycheck towards your own retirement account.
         3. Some companies may also offer a set amount (known as a match) based on what you put towards your retirement account.
         4. The amount of money that can be put into retirement accounts may be limited on your income and other restrictions from the government and/or your company.
   b. Named for the section of the tax code that describes them.
   c. **401k or 403b**
      i. Most common type of defined contribution plans
      ii. **401k** - usually used for private companies.
      iii. **403b** - usually used for government institutions and nonprofit companies.
      iv. Both come in two types: **Traditional and Roth.**

1. **Traditional 401k or 403b accounts**
   a. **Money placed in the account:**
      i. Pre-tax: taxes are not paid on the money placed into these accounts.
      ii. Match: some companies have matching programs that can increase your retirement account.
   b. **Money taken out of the account:**
      i. Money must be taken out after age 59 ½ and before 70 ½ so that no penalties are assessed.
      ii. If money is taken out before age 59 ½, income taxes and will be charged a 10% penalty.
      iii. Money is taxed at your marginal tax rate at the time the money is removed.

2. **Roth 401k and 403b accounts**
   a. **Money placed in the account:**
      i. After-tax: you pay taxes on the money before it is placed in the account.
      ii. Match: some companies have matching programs that can increase your retirement account.
      iii. It grows tax free.
   b. **Money taken out of the account:**
      i. You can start taking money out of this account, penalty free, at age 59 ½.
      ii. There is no age when money must be taken out of the account.
      iii. These accounts can be handed down to children or grandchildren.
      iv. Money is removed tax free.

3. **457 - also called "Deferred Compensation" plans**
   a. Offered by some companies either as a sole retirement plan or in addition to a 401K or 403b.
   b. **Money placed into the account:**
      i. Pre-tax: taxes are not paid on the money placed in the account.
      ii. Companies **can not add** to the amount, in most cases.

c. **Money taken out of the account:**
 i. Money can be taken out when you leave the company.
  1. Understand what options you have before you invest.
 ii. Some companies have rules that
  1. Force you to take money out of these accounts when you leave the company, or
  2. Allow you to roll over your 457 to another company without penalty, or
  3. Allow you to roll your 457 into a roll over IRA.
  4. Money is taxed at the tax rate at the time the money is removed.

3. **Personal Retirement Plans**

 a. **Individual Retirement Arrangements (IRA)**
  i. These come in two types as well: **Traditional and Roth**

  1. **Traditional IRA**
   a. **Money placed into the account**
    i. Pre-tax money.
     1. There are income limits as to who can place money into the accounts for the pre-tax benefits.
     2. <u>Single person for 2013:</u>
      a. < $58k - full deduction.
      b. $58k to $68 - phased out deduction.
      c. > $69 - no deduction.
    ii. You must earn the money through a job to contribute to the account.
     1. You can't use savings or gifts to fund this account.
     2. If you are married, you can use your spouse's income to fund your account.
    iii. Maximum amount you can put into this account each year:
     1. $5,500 if less than 50 years old.
     2. $6,500 if 50 years old or older

   b. **Money taken out of the account:**
    i. Money must be taken out after age 59 ½ and before 70 ½ so that no penalties are assessed.
    ii. If money is taken out before age 59 ½, income taxes and will be charged a 10% penalty.
    iii. Money is taxed at your tax rate at the time the money is removed.

2. **Roth IRA**
   a. **Money placed into the account;**
      i. After-tax money (no tax deduction for using these accounts)
      ii. You must earn the money through a job to contribute to the account.
         1. You can't use savings or gifts to fund this account.
         2. If you are married, you can use your spouses income as a source of income and fund your account
      iii. There are **income limits** as to who can place money into the accounts.
   b. **Money taken out of the account:**
      i. Roth IRAs offer some special provisions to take out the money, without penalty, before you turn 59 ½.
      ii. There is no age limit when the money must be taken out.
      iii. It grows tax free.
3. **Simplified Employee Pension Plans (SEP-IRAs)**
   a. Used by self-employed individuals and small-business owners to save for retirement
   b. Because this is used as a sole retirement account, up to $50,000/year can be contributed to these accounts.
   c. **Money placed into the account:**
      i. Pre-tax money
      ii. You must earn the money through your own business.
   d. **Money taken out of the account:**
      i. Money must be taken out after age 59 ½ and before 70 ½.
      ii. If money is taken out before 59 ½, income taxes and a 10% penalty will be charged.
      iii. Money is taxed at your tax rate at the time the money is removed.
4. **Investment Options**
   a. Once you have the account, you have to determine how to invest the money that is placed in the account.
   b. Depending on which investment company you use for your retirement accounts, you will have different options for how the money is invested.
   c. Many investment companies offer a variety of different products in which to invest your money:
      i. Cash Accounts
      ii. Money Market Accounts
      iii. Bonds
      iv. Mutual Funds
      v. Stocks

      vi. Exchange Traded Funds (ETF)
- d. How you invest is dependent on:
  - i. Your goals for your accounts.
  - ii. Your risk tolerance.
  - iii. Other savings and investments you may have.
- e. Set up an appointment with a representative from the investment company to review your options.
- f. <u>If you have no idea where to start:</u>
  - i. Start investing into a S&P 500 index mutual fund.
  - ii. This is a starting point to get you going until you can learn how to allocate your retirement investment.

5. **How Much Should You Save for Retirement?**
   - a. Most Financial Gurus (MFG) suggest people save 10-20% of their pre-tax money in retirement accounts.
     - i. 10% is a good starting point, however, you should calculate how much you think you will need.
   - b. This is where the "Pay yourself first" phrase comes from. "Pay" money from your paycheck, to your retirement account, before any other bills are paid.
   - c. **Calculating the amount needed for retirement:**
     - i. Start with the amount of money you want to withdraw from your retirement accounts each month to live.
       1. Typically, it is assumed that you will need only 85% of your current income, because:
          - a. You will not be paying a mortgage (this is assumed that it will be paid off).
          - b. You will not have to save for retirement (because you are in retirement).
     - ii. However, some expenses can increase, such as travel and health care expenses.
     - iii. MFG recommend that you start your withdraw rate from your retirement savings at four percent annually, then increase that amount by 3% to account for inflation.
     - iv. Four percent is used because most gurus assume that your retirement account should be earning 8-10% compounded interest.
     - v. With a conservative withdraw rate of 4%, the money will still grow, even though money is being withdrawn.

vi. Saving for Retirement Example

1. John currently earns $4,000 a month.

   a. **Step One: Calculate expected Needed Income**

      i. Income of $4,000/month which is $48,000/year

      ii. $4,000 x 0.85 = $3,400 (85% of current income)

      iii. $3,400 x 12 months = $40,800 annually (85% of current income)

   b. **Step Two: Calculate total amount needed in retirement accounts to achieve this**

      1. $40,800 / 0.04% = $1,020,000 needed in a retirement account at the start of retirement

vii. "Back of the Envelope" Calculation:

1. John could have also used this quick approximation:

   a. Total monthly income replacement wanted in retirement: $4,000

   b. Figure the annual "salary": $4,000 x 12 = $48,000

   c. Multiple the income wanted by 25: $48,000 x 25 = $1,200,000

   d. As you can see, although it is $180k different than the prior calculation (because there isn't a 15% decrease), it gives you a rough approximation of the scale of the retirement account needed to achieve this level of income in retirement.

6. Resources

   i. The Bogleheads' Guide to Retirement Planning by Larimore, Lindauer, Ferri, Dogu, and Bogle.

   ii. www.MoneyChimp.com

Chapter 12
Epilogue to Section #1: The Basics of Personal Finance

This is the end of Section #1: The Basics of Personal Finance.

I hope this has provided a good base on which to build your knowledge in personal finance as we delve into more complex and specific issues relevant to you in your current and future career.

In the next section, we will learn about **The Residency Years**.

We will take what we learned in Section #1, and apply it to the life of a Resident Physician. It is during your residency and fellowship training that you will develop good skills and habits to follow the rest of your career. Hopefully, good personal financial management will be one of those.

Section # 2: The Residency Years

Chapter 13
Introduction to The Residency Years

Transitions can be stressful. The key to managing stressful life transitions is to plan ahead of time, follow through with the plan, and make adjustments as needed. If things are not going to plan, don't panic . . . *"No battle plan ever survives contact with the enemy."*

You will be going through several major transitions during your training:

1. Medical school to residency
2. Residency to fellowship (possibly)
3. Residency/fellowship to independent practice

Transitions can be an exciting time and a little scary. However, there are some steps you can take to make the transition smoother and less likely upset your financial plan. This section is dedicated to guiding you through those first few transitions of your career.

Chapter 14
Paperwork Needed for Residency

Once you have been accepted into residency, there are a number of documents you will be required to have before starting residency.

1. **Physician in Training (PIT) Permit**
   a. Once you have finished medical school, you will need a license to practice medicine.
      i. During residency training, most residents start with a PIT, because they have not completed Step 3 of the USMLE/COMLEX and, therefore, are unable to obtain a medical license.
   b. Until you have your own state license, you will need a PIT permit to practice medicine.
      1. A State medical permit allows you to practice medicine while you are in a training program.
      2. You can only "practice" medicine at the institution where you are a resident/fellow.
      3. You will need to use your institution's DEA number to prescribe controlled substances.
      4. Your residency/fellowship program will be able to help you obtain this document well before your start date.
         a. It is critical that you start work on this as soon as possible.
      5. Do not let this permit lapse or you may need to take leave from your training program, until the issue is resolved.
         a. Most PITs will last for the duration of your residency, but if you switch residencies, or do a fellowship, you may need to apply once again.

2. **Letter of Agreement or Letter of Acceptance**
   a. This can be a simple document that states you have accepted the resident/fellow position at your new institution.
   b. This could also be a complex document that reads much like a contract.

3. **Employment Contract:**
   a. Although you are still in training, you are also an employee.
   b. These resident/fellow contracts are standardized but you still need to read every word and save a copy of it for your records.
   c. **What you should expect in the contents** (not an inclusive list):
      i. **Type of Residency** (Family Practice, Pediatrics, Anesthesiology, etc.)
      ii. **Duration of the Contract**
         1. One year is standard. You will be signing a new contract every year.
      iii. **Stipend** (also known as your salary)

    iv. Responsibilities and expectations:
1. Conditions for re-appointment / promotion
2. Required Licensure / Permits
3. Work Hours
4. Mandatory Training
5. Immunizations (yes, there are required immunizations at most institutions)
6. Drug Screening
7. Background Check

    v. Benefits Provided (other than salary):
1. Time off
2. Sick leave
3. Disability Benefits (usually not very good, but at least it is something)
4. Health Insurance
5. Education Fund

    vi. Grounds for dismissal from the training program and non-renewal of your contract

    vii. Professional Liability Insurance information
1. Terms of your Medical Malpractice Insurance
   a. Most residencies / fellowships provide this for you.

4. **Financial Implications of this Paperwork**
   a. **PIT**
      i. This will cost you some time and money to obtain.
      ii. Figure in the cost of this permit so it can be worked into your budget.
   b. **Your Contract**
      i. This will include your salary and how often you will be paid.
         1. This is vital for trying to figure out a budget and the size and extent of housing you can afford.

Chapter 15
Financial Implications of the Medical School to Resident Transition

There are multiple financial issues to be addressed during the transition from medical school to residency.

1. **Medical School Loans**
    i.   Usually during your last week of medical school, you are given a "debriefing" on your loans.
    ii. Find out from your lender when you need to start paying back your loans.
        1. Most lenders will give you a 6 month grace period from the time you graduate from medical school. (You don't have to start paying on your loan for 6 months)
    iii. Start looking into all of your options for how to payback your loans.
        1. You need to know if you are going to start making payments, defer your loan, or put your loan into forbearance at the end of this 6 month grace period.
    iv. A complete discussion of this process can be found later in the chapter on *Managing vs. Treating Medical School Loans.*

2. **Potential Loss of Health Insurance**
    i.   Make sure you understand your options as to how to maintain your health insurance coverage.
    ii. Some plans allow for retrospective premium payments to activate your insurance, should something happen while you are in-between med school and residency.
        1. This would be a cost effective way to maintain your health insurance and do it cheaply.
        2. **How it works:**
            a. When you graduate, you stop paying your health insurance, because you are no longer a student.
            b. If you are sick or injured, then you pay the premium, and the insurance company treats you as if you continued to pay all along.
        3. Before you decide to do this, get this in writing.
        4. It would probably be better to pay for the few months of coverage, before you start residency, to make sure you are covered against catastrophic injuries.

3. **Moving Expenses**
   a. Hold on to all your receipts, because the cost of the move may be tax deductible.
      i. If you move > 50 miles for work, then you can deduct the cost of the move from your federal taxes.
      ii. Moving across the state, or to another state can be a pricey endeavor.
   b. Keep in mind you will need **deposits for:**
      i. New apartment
      ii. Telephone
      iii. Utilities
      iv. Cable service

4. **Loss of "Income"**
   a. You will graduate mid-May and will not have a paycheck from residency until sometime in July/August.
   b. The last amount of money from your medical school loans may run out, since you will still need to pay living expenses during this time.

5. **Funding your Transition**
   a. Ideally you have been saving money for the transition period, but if you are "normal" then you have not.
   b. **Your options (from most desirable to least):**
      i. Live off money that **you have been setting aside** for the transition period.
      ii. **Live with family and/or friends** to make the money stretch.
      iii. Live off the last of your **loan money.**
      iv. Some lenders offer **private residency relocation loans.**
         1. Used to cover living/moving expenses
         2. These loans tend to have high interest rates (8-10%).
            a. They may have a grace period where no payments are required.
            b. These are your first priority to pay off as quickly as possible after you start earning an income.
      v. **Use a credit card to "float" the expenses.**
         1. The most expensive way (and potentially the riskiest way) to fund your transition.
            a. High interest rates, and potential for even higher increases if payments can not be made.

6. **Resident Housing**
   a. Renting vs. buying a home while in residency:
      i. There are a number of different factors that go into this decision, however, you should at least consider renting.

1. You will have even **less time and less control over your schedule** than when you were in medical school.
   a. When (not if) the refrigerator, air-conditioner, or plumbing breaks, who will be able to stay at home to wait on the repairs?
   b. When things do break, how will you pay for them?
2. Residency is at least 3 years long and you may have to move when it is done.
3. **What about the "vast amounts of riches" from real estate?**
   a. When my wife and I bought our home at the start of residency, we were thinking that we would make a profit on it when we sold it.
      i. We would have come out ahead, but we had to replace the air-conditioning/heating unit, the plumbing needed repair, and there were various other repairs we needed to complete for the home livable.)
   b. If you do need to move for fellowship/work, trying to sell a home during residency is very difficult, and it might not sell as easily as you think.
   c. Do you really want to be a landlord in a different town, or state if you have to move and rent it out?

b. **Residency is a time for focusing on your training.**
   i. Owning a home, particularly if you are single, can be a large stress and drain on your resources.
   ii. Doing even routine maintenance can be time consuming during a season in your life when you should be learning your trade.
   iii. I don't even recommend home purchase for new faculty when they start their first job. (*see Chapter 30: Home Ownership for the New Staff Physician*)
      1. The main reason for this is a home can be a big distraction.
         a. You only have a short period of time to be in training for your career.
            i. If you are worried about repairs, it is hard to focus on your residency.

c. **If you decide to buy a home during residency, consider the following:**
   i. **Figure out your budget before buying a home.**
      1. Use caution when looking for housing.
         a. The three most expensive things in a budget are:
            i. Housing
            ii. Utilities
            iii. Transportation
      2. Most mortgage companies will offer you a larger home than you can comfortably afford.

3. Most homes will cost about 5%-10% of the cost of the home to maintain it.
   a. So a $140,000 home will cost between $7,000 and $15,000 a year to operate, including utilities, maintenance, and taxes.
   b. Most finance gurus recommend your housing be no more than 25-35% of your take home pay.
      i. This can be very difficult (if not impossible) in expensive housing markets.
4. Review *Chapters 5: Home Mortgages*
   a. Make sure that your resident salary will support the type of home that is available in the area where you want to live.
   b. Do your own calculations as to how much home you can afford.

ii. For some families, owning a home is less stressful than renting, particularly if there are children or pets involved.

iii. When you own a home, it also ties you to a community, which is a good thing.
   1. However, I have seen residents who stay in the same place for fellowship or work, even though there are better programs and opportunities elsewhere, partially because they own a home there.

d. **Doctor Loans**
   i. Beware of "Doctor Loans".
      1. Anything with the title "Doctor" in it can be a targeted attempt to play on your ego and may give you a poor deal.
   ii. Doctor Loans for home mortgages usually do not require any money down, may/may not require PMI, and may/may not have other fees and costs associated with them.
   iii. Compare these loans to other "standard" loans to see if they are a better or worse loan.

e. **Emergency Fund**
   i. Before you buy your home, you should have your emergency fund in place (3-6 months of expenses) and have the seller provide a home warranty which will cover repairs in the home for that 1st year.

Chapter 16
The Checklist for Medical School Seniors and New Graduates

1. **Before you Leave Medical School**
   - ☐ Know the terms of your student loans and how to contact the lending company.
     - ☐ Review when your grace period ends.
   - ☐ Give your medical school your new address information in case they need to contact you.

2. **Paperwork for New Residency**
   - ☐ Keep in constant contact with your new residency.
   - ☐ Paperwork for Residency
     - ☐ Letter of Acceptance in place
     - ☐ PIT permit in place for your state
     - ☐ Employment Contract signed

3. **Plan for your gap in Health Insurance.**

4. **Build Your Budgets**
   - ☐ Use a medical school budget for the rest of your medical school training.
   - ☐ How are you planning on funding the transition between Medical School and Residency?
   - ☐ Design your residency budget based on your new take home salary.
     - ☐ Monthly
     - ☐ Annual

5. **Plan your Housing**
   - ☐ Based on your residency budget, determine where you are going to live.
   - ☐ Try to be conservative, so that you can start to pay down school loans.
   - ☐ Consider renting during your residency to simplify your life.

Chapter 17
Basic Resident Finance

Now that you are a "real" doctor, people will assume that you are "rich". If they don't think you are rich, then they will assume "you will be rich" when you finish residency. People will tell you what you can afford, but they will never tell you what you can't afford. (And they will never know your salary.)

1. **Resident Finance Pearls**
   a. **Use your residency years to learn how to manage your finances.**
      i. This is the time during your training to learn how to manage your finances, because the concepts of personal finance are similar between when you are a resident and when you become faculty. What changes is the size and scope of your finances.

   b. **Earn like a resident, live like a medical student.**
      i. Every year, I know when July rolls around because of the flock of brand new BMWs, Lexus, and Mercedes that are in the resident parking garage.
      ii. Resist the temptation to buy a new car and spring for eating out a lot. It is amazing how quickly your take home pay can be spent.

   c. **Speaking of salary . . .**
      i. Do yourself a favor, don't complain about:
         1. How little you think you are making.
         2. How much you are earning an hour.
      ii. The nurses, techs, and other staff may be earning less than you and it is an insult to them for you to complain about how little you make.
         1. Most other workers in a hospital will show you no sympathy and it will only anger them when you complain.
         2. You are paying a price to be a physician, suck it up.
         3. You are earning the median income.

   d. **Beware of the "Doctor Loans"**
      i. Aways review the information twice before applying for a "Doctor Loan".
         1. Compare it to other loans to see if it is a good deal for you.
      ii. Because you have a MD/DO after your name, you have a target on you.

   e. **Automate your financial life**
         1. Put all your bills on auto-draft or on a credit card.
            a. Pay off your credit cards every month.
            b. In fact, put the credit card on auto-draft.
         2. You wont' have to spend precious free time paying bills.

2. **Resident Monthly Budget**
    a. With the information from your resident contract, start working through a monthly budget.
        i.   If you know your salary, you should be able to calculate your monthly / 2 week salary.
            1.   ex: $50,000 is a gross income of $4,166.67 monthly or $1,923.08 every two weeks.
            2.   You will then need to figure that you will have taxes, heath insurance, and other deductions removed, which will reduce this **gross income** to your **net income.**
            3.   Contact your institution's House Staff Office to help you determine what your take home paycheck will be.
            4.   Use *Chapter 1* in the first section of this book to review how to build a budget.
    b. When you get your first paycheck, rework your budget to bring it into the "real world".
    c. Build your budget to determine how much debt you can pay off.
        i.   Start by paying off any relocation loans or credit card debt.
            1.   Pay minimum payments on all the loans, and attack the smallest loan with a vengeance.
        ii. Evaluate your other private loans to see if you can pay these back as well.
        iii. See discussion on Income Based Repayment (IBR) in *Medical School Loans Chapter 19.*
    d. Resident Budget Busters
        i.   Usually, it isn't the large purchases that get residents into trouble. It's the many small purchases that add up.
        ii. It amazes me how many residents buy their lunch each day.
            1.   Fancy coffee, eating out, and buying lunch tend to be the big culprits.

3. **Broad Annual Budget for the Resident**
   a. This should be an annual map to know when expenses will be coming up.
      i. The broad budget for you as a resident runs as an academic year does: July through June.
      ii. Include both personal and professional expenses that you are expecting to have during the year.
      iii. See Example at Right

PGY -2 Year Example	
July	Professional Dues
August	Medical License Application
September	
October	
November	
December	Christmas Gifts
January	
February	
March	Car State Inspection Due
April	Car License Due
May	
June	Application for Boards

4. **Emergency Fund for Residents**
   a. Start with an emergency fund equal to one month of expenses.
      i. You will know this based on your monthly budget you have set up.
      ii. Once all of your credit cards and other loans (excluding your education debt) are paid off, then expand your emergency fund to 6 months of expenses.

5. **Insurance**
   a. Auto Insurance
      i. Make sure your auto insurance is up to date.
   b. Health Insurance
      i. Check your coverage that you have on your health insurance.
   c. Life Insurance
      i. If you have a family or have people that rely on you for your financial support, obtain life insurance.
   d. Disability Insurance
      i. Start looking into disability insurance and get a basic policy in place, before you become injured or ill.
         1. This is the time for you to get **long term, own occupation disability insurance** in place.
         2. You will only be able to get a policy that will cover what you are currently earning, but obtain a policy that allows for future increases when your salary goes up.

    ii. Review the *Disability Insurance section in Chapter 3.*

  e. Check with your professional organizations to see if you can get a discount on your life or disability insurance.

6. **Residents and Taxes**
   a. You may be able to deduct the cost of moving (if greater than 50 miles) if it was for a job.
      i. You would only be able to deduct this amount if you itemize your deductions and hold on to all of your receipts.
   b. As stated in *Chapter 4,* I recommend doing your own taxes at least the first few years so that you learn how to file a tax return.
   c. The commercially available software is relatively inexpensive and easy to use.
      i. As with other parts of your training, residency is a good time to learn how these basic things work.

7. **Maximizing your Education / Travel Fund as a Resident**
   a. Plan to use this fund wisely to maximize this benefit.
      i. Find out what you can spend it on:
         a. Travel to conferences, books, and review courses
         b. USMLE/COMLEX exams, medical licensure, and board certification exams
      ii. Find out if it carries over each year
         a. If it carries over, you could save it for larger expenses later in your residency training, such as board exams and review courses.
   b. Learn which forms, receipts, and other paperwork/requirements are needed in order to use your education fund.
   c. Please see *Chapter 32: Managing your Education Fund,* regarding a much larger discussion on education/travel fund.

8. **Other Resident Employee Benefits**
   a. Talk with upper level residents to maximize your benefits.
      i. Free meals while on call?
      ii. Family meals while on call?
      iii. Department funds to help with abstract presentations?
   b. Are there other benefits for being an employee?
      i. Discounts on cell phones?
      ii. Gym memberships?
      iii. Discount on other goods/services?
   c. Try to maximize all your benefits.

9. **Resident Retirement**
   a. It's a good idea to start saving for retirement in residency.
   b. Please see *Chapter 20: Retirement Savings for Residents.*

Chapter 18
Advanced Resident Finance

Your needs will change as you transition through your training.
Below is a basic framework of what kinds of residency expenses you can expect to encounter.

1. **Post Graduate Year One (Intern Year)**
   a. Consider taking your USMLE Step 3/COMLEX Part 3 exam as soon as you can.
      i. This is a two day exam.
         1. You will need to work with your department to schedule the time for this exam.
      ii. It will **cost ~ $750 - $900 to take the exam.**
         1. When budgeting for the exam, consider the costs of taking the exam and any related review materials that you may need.
      iii. Some states require you to have a minimum number of months in a training program before you take this exam.
      iv. Some programs require that you pass it by a certain time in your training or you will be **fired from the program**.
      v. The further into your specialized training you go, the harder it is to remember some of the general medical information from medical school.
      vi. Even if you don't plan on getting a Full Medical License until later, get this exam out of the way.
      vii. It's very unlikely you will have "more time" later in residency. There is no benefit to waiting to take the exam.

2. **Upper Level Residency Years**
   a. **Medical License:**
      i. Depending on when you are planning to graduate, start working on your application for your Full Medical License in the state or states you plan to work.
         1. State specific requirements with costs:
            a. http://www.fsmb.org/usmle_eliinitial.html
      ii. You will need a State Medical License, DPS number and DEA number to practice on your own.
      iii. Costs Involved:
         1. Medical License application fee
         2. Medical school transcript fee
         3. DPS application fee
         4. DEA application fee

iv. **Time Frame for Medical Licensure**
1. Give yourself enough time to obtain your medical license.
   a. It can take 6-12 months to get a state medical license.
2. Obtaining DEA and DPS numbers can also take several months.

   a. **Reciprocality**
      i. It is much easier to obtain a medical license in another state if you have a current license in your home state.
      ii. Even if you don't know where you want to practice, obtaining a medical license in your current state might help you down the line.
      iii. This can become expensive, so if you know in which state you want to practice, then apply there.
      iv. Universal applications can be helpful if you are applying to multiple states:
         1. http://www.fsmb.org/ua.html

   b. **Continued Maintenance**
      i. Once you obtain your Medical License and your DEA/DPS numbers, you will need to renew them every 2 years.
         1. This has a recurring cost with it as well.
      ii. If these lapse, you could potentially lose the ability to work as a physician, until they are once again current.
         1. It can also be more expensive to reapply for licensure during the lapsed period.
      iii. Continuing Medical Education (CME) is usually not an issue during residency and fellowship.

   c. **Track Expiration Dates**
      i. Keep a master list of when your medical license, certifications, etc. expire, so you can renew them well ahead of the deadlines.
      ii. Also, keep a master copy of your initial licensure because you will be asked for this information on credentialing applications (see below).

   d. **Caveats**
      i. When you obtain a full medical license during residency is up to you.
      ii. Some specialty boards have a "hard stop" that will not allow you to progress in the testing until you have a full license.

3. **Senior Year of Residency**
    a. **Medical License:**
        i.   If you have not obtained your full license, do it now.
             1. Having to post-pone your job, your credentials and your board certification because you don't have a medical license is a bad way to spend your post graduation time.
    b. **Board Certification Exams:**
        i.   Each specialty is different in the timing of application deadlines and exam dates.
        ii. Find out when you need to apply for your boards and how much they will cost.
             1. Some board certifications will require you to pay for the first part of your exam when you are still a resident.
             2. Also figure in the cost of board preparation material.
                 a. This can be a significant cost.
             3. Also figure in the cost of travel for the exam.
                 a. Plane tickets, hotels, meals, etc.

Chapter 19
Managing vs. Treating Medical School Loans

It is your responsibility to learn everything you can about your loans. Below is a brief guide to common Medical School Loans. Each situation is unique. Contact your loan company to get specific information based on your specific loans and the agreements you signed.

1. **Why Even Consider Paying Off Your Medical School Loans Early?**

   Many authors recommend ways to avoid paying your loans to stretch out the payments as long as possible. This came from a time when interest rates on medical school loans were around 1.5%. Now, most loans are in the range of 6%, which makes them less desirable to maintain over a long period of time.

   Some residents may still avoid paying their loans during residency, because they believe they will be "earning real money" when they become staff physicians and can pay on their loans then.

   I strongly encourage you to start paying off your debt as soon as possible. Instead of "managing" your medical school loans, please consider "treating" your loans and get a cure from the debt that you built up to become a physician.

2. **Organize your loans**
   a. Keep track of how **much you owe and to whom you owe it**.
   b. Track which **type of loans** you have:
      i. Federal Family Education Loan Program
      ii. Federal Stafford Loans
      iii. Federal PLUS loans
      iv. Private Loans

      v. **Government Loans**
         1. Which loans are subsidized? (interest was paid during your medical school)
         2. Which loans are unsubsidized? (interest started accruing the moment you took out the loan)
   c. Find out from your lender/lenders **when you need to start paying on your loans.**
      i. During medical school, you have been on loan deferment.
      ii. Most lenders give you a **6 month grace period** from the time you graduate from medical school before you must start paying back your loans.
      iii. Calculate if **loan consolidation** is a good idea for you.
         1. Multiple loans are combined into one loan by the lender.
         2. This can reduce your monthly payment, however, you may pay more interest over the life of the loan.
         3. There are restrictions on which loans can be consolidated.

        4. You will need to discuss with your lender if this will save you money.

    iv. Learn which loans

        1. Will be **forgiven in the event of your death** (Stafford)

        2. **Can be forgiven through federal programs** (Federal Direct)

        3. **You need to attack with a vengeance** (high interest rates from a private lender).

    v. Find out if there is a prepayment penalty should you want to pay off the loan early.

        1. It is unusual to have this, but it can happen.

3. Calculate your Monthly Payment.

    a. Government Loans have different options for their repayment

      i. <u>Standard Repayment Plan:</u>

        a. Pay the full amount due each month

        b. The loan is paid off over 10 years.

        c. May not be possible to do based on a resident salary.

        d. Most residents see this standard plan, get overwhelmed, decide they can't make any payments, then postpone payments as long as possible.

      ii. <u>Graduated Repayment Plan:</u>

        a. Start with lower payments, then they increase (every 2 years).

        b. You pay off the loan over 10 years.

      iii. <u>Extended Repayment Plan:</u>

        a. Payments are either fixed or graduated over the payback period.

        b. You pay the loan off over 12-25 years.

      iv. <u>Income-Contingent Repayment:</u>

        1. Payments are calculated each year based on:

          a. Your family income

          b. Your family size

          c. How much you owe on the loans

        2. You can pay the loan off over 25 years.

      v. <u>Income-Sensitive Repayment Plan:</u>

        1. Monthly payments are based on your annual salary.

        2. You pay the loan off over 10 years.

vi. Income Based Repayment (IBR):

1. Perhaps the best repayment option for residents
2. Your monthly loan repayment bill is made more affordable based on your salary.
3. For most lenders, you must start repayment within your 6 month grace period after medical school to be eligible.
4. By using this plan and paying on your student loans during residency, you may be eligible for Public Service Loan Forgiveness (see below *Public Service Loan Forgiveness*).

5. **How is the Income Based Repayment calculated?**
   a. Based on the poverty level guidelines, which can be found at http://aspe.hhs.gov/POVERTY/
   b. Find the poverty guidelines based on your state and number of people in your family and multiply by 1.5. Subtract this number from your Adjusted Gross Income (AGI comes from your tax return), then multiply this number by 0.15 and divide by 12 to get your monthly payment. (What???) See the two boxes below.
      i. What if you don't have a AGI, because you have not paid taxes while you where in medical school?
         1. Contact your loan servicer, but they will probably use your estimated AGI based on your resident salary.

IBR Example #1: The single resident with an AGI of $45,000

Poverty Level is $11,170 x 1.5 = $16,755
If AGI is estimated at $45,000 then $45,000-$16,755 = $28,245
this is the "discretionary income" then $28,245 x 0.15 = $4,236.75
$4,236.75 / 12 months = $353.06 = your monthly payments

IBR Example #2: The married resident with an AGI of $100,000

Poverty Level is $15,130 x1.5 = $22,695
(higher poverty level because of a family of 2)
If AGI is estimated at $100,000 then $100,000 - $22,695 = $77,305
this is the "discretionary income" then $77,305 x 0.15 = $11,595.75
$11,595.75 / 12 months = $966.31 = your monthly payment

4. **Postponing your Loan Repayment**
    a. Here are your options, if you decide to postpose paying on your medical school debt during residency:
        i. **Loan Deferment**
            1. Available for some loans for various reasons
            2. Historically, residents could claim economic hardship. However, with current resident salaries, it is more difficult to do this.
            3. Under some circumstances, you will only be able to **defer your loan for up to 3 years.**
                a. Interest is "paid" by the US government on subsidized loans.
                b. Interest accumulates on unsubsidized loans.
        ii. **Forbearance**
            1. More stringent requirements compared to Loan Deferment
            2. You are able to delay paying on your loans for **up to 12 months.**
            3. Interest continues to **accumulate on subsidized and unsubsidized loans.**
            4. <u>Discretionary Forbearance</u> - lender decides if you can go into forbearance.
            5. <u>Mandatory Forbearance</u> - you meet certain criteria for postponed repayments
    b. **Several myths residents give for not starting to pay back loans**
        i. <u>I want to keep my loans as long as possible because the loans are forgiven, if I die.</u>
            1. At age 32, you are 4 times more likely to become disabled than die.
            2. If you are disabled and can't work as a physician to pay back your loans then you have a huge debt and a small possibility of ever getting out of debt.
        ii. <u>I can make more money with investing than paying the interest rate on my loans. Its free money!</u>
            1. This was the case when interest rates were at an all time low of around 1.5%
            2. All investing requires a risk/benefit ratio to be evaluated.
            3. If you pay off your loans on time or early, then it is one less payment that needs to be made.
        iii. <u>I'll have more money later when I am a staff physician and the payment will be much easier when I have a much better income.</u>
            1. This is assuming that physician salaries don't change, you are still able to work as a physician in your chosen specialty, and your life situation doesn't change.

5. **Why Start to Pay Off Loans in Residency?**
    a. You owe the money.
    b. It starts to build the habit of paying off your debts.
        i. You should be forming good habits during your residency that last a lifetime.
    c. You are making good money now as a resident, put it to work.
        i. The median US income is approximately $46k.
    d. The interest that you pay on your loan is tax deductible when you are a resident, less likely as staff.
        i. **Residents may be able to deduct up to $2,500 of the interest payments on loans each year.**
            1. If you earn less than $60k ($120k if filing as a married couple), then you can deduct up to $2,500 of interest on your loans.
            2. If you earn $60k - $70k ($120k - $150k as a married couple), then you can deduct a prorated amount of the interest.
            3. If you earn >$70k ($150k if filing as a married couple), then you can not deduct any of the interest.
        ii. For most physicians, they will **only be able to realize this tax advantage while they are a resident.**
    e. By starting to pay on your loans during residency, you have the potential to maximize your government loan benefits.
        i. If you start paying on your loans during residency, you could have some of the money completely forgiven within a few years of working as faculty for a qualified employer. (See *Public Loan Forgiveness Program* below for a detailed explanation.)

6. **Public Loan Forgiveness Program**
    a. The outstanding balance on the loan is forgiven after paying monthly payments for ten years (no matter the repayment schedule).
        i. To qualify, you must work for a **government institution or a non-profit company** during the time of repayment.
        ii. **Available for Direct Loans only**
            1. If you have other loans, you can consolidate them into a Direct Consolidation Loan to take advantage of the program (http://www.loanconsolidation.ed.gov/).

b. **How would this work for you?**

Example of IBR and Public Loan Forgiveness:

<u>Pediatric Resident, who wants to do a fellowship in Hem-Onc, and do academic medicine.</u>
Pediatric Residency = 3 years (uses IBR to make payments)
Hem-Onc fellowship = 3 years (uses IBR to make payments)
Staff at a University = 4 years (pays full payments because of salary)

In the end, the physician paid 6 years of lower payments and 4 years of full payments towards the loans, then the outstanding loans were forgiven.

---

c. **How do you find out about this benefit?**
   i. Contact your lender and find out if you have a Direct Loan or if you can consolidate into a Direct Loan.
   ii. Find out if the loan forgiveness is considered a taxable event.
       1. A loan forgiveness as a taxable event means that whatever amount of the loan was forgiven is considered "income" by the IRS and you would be assessed a tax bill.
       2. Having a government loan forgiven as a taxable event is rare.
           a. Even if it is a taxable event, it is less expensive than paying off the entire loan with principal and interest.

d. Based on your resident monthly budget, see if IBR is an option for you.
   i. If you start paying on your loans, and end up having a shorter training period, then you are getting the benefit of the tax deduction and making some progress towards your loans.
   ii. If you have a longer training period (5 or more years), rework your budget till you are able to cut your lifestyle to make it happen.
   iii. Because of cost of living in some areas of the country, IBR still might not be an option for you.

7. **Resources**
   a. http://studentaid.ed.gov/
   b. http://www.loanconsolidation.ed.gov/

Chapter 20
Retirement Savings for Residents
"I wished I had not had saved so much for retirement!" said no one ever.

1. **Reasons Residents Give Why They Don't Saving for Retirement in Residency.**
   a. They don't have enough money to save for retirement.
   b. They will be earning much more money later and therefore, any amount of money they save during residency will be small in comparison.
   c. They don't have time to learn about retirement savings.

2. **Reasons to Start Saving for Retirement.**
   a. Residency is a time to instill good habits that will last a lifetime . . . including saving for retirement.
      i. Residency is also a time to learn new skills, including how retirement accounts work.
   b. The compounding interest that you will be earning on the money will add to your retirement nest egg, even with the relatively short period of time of residency.
   c. As a staff physician, you will become limited as to the amount of money you can save in retirement accounts.
      i. If you are a higher earning physician, you may not be able to put the standard recommendation of 15% of your income into your retirement account because of phase out rules.
      ii. Your higher income may prevent you from contributing to certain accounts.
         1. For example, if you earn more than $127k (as a single person) or $188k (as a married couple) you are not eligible to contribute to a Roth IRA.
            a. There is a way around this, but your options tend to decrease with higher income brackets.
            b. Please see *Chapter 29: Staff Physician Retirement Planning.*
   d. You never know how your financial situation may change.
      i. If illness or tragedy strikes, you may not be working as a staff physician as long as you had anticipated, therefore you will not have as many years to contribute to your retirement accounts.
   e. As a medical school student, you have already missed out on funding your retirement account for four years.

3. **How to Start Saving for Retirement**
   a. As a general rule, you should be saving at least 10%-15% of your gross income towards retirement.
   b. Start with something . . . 5% is better than no retirement savings.
   c. Start with your employee retirement plan offered by your residency.
      i. Start with your 401k/403b.
         1. Some residencies offer a matching program; take advantage of this free money.
      ii. If a 457 is offered, make sure you know what your options are after you leave residency.
         1. Are you forced to cash it out or can you roll over to another 457, or roll to an IRA?
   d. Start your retirement savings with your first paycheck, and you won't miss the money.
   e. Once your employee retirement is maxed out, and you want to save more, open a Roth IRA and invest your money there.
      i. Although you will not get the benefit of the pre-tax tax deduction, a Roth IRA gives you some options that a traditional IRA does not.
         1. Also, most physicians will be at an income level that does not allow them to contribute to Roth IRAs easily.
   f. Review *Chapter 11* for a detailed explanation of different retirement account options.

4. **How to Start Investing your Retirement Money**
   a. There are many books out there on retirement investing, but a simple strategy is to start investing in a index Growth Stock Mutual Fund like a **S&P 500 index fund.**
   b. Start putting money there and then research where you want to invest.
   c. Get some free help with your retirement:
      i. The company managing your employee or IRA retirement account (Vanguard, Fidelity, etc.) will have representatives to help you with your retirement options.
      ii. The Human Resources (HR) department can also help you contact the right person.

5. **Resources for Investing:**
   a. The Boggleheads' Guide to Investing by Larimore, Lindauer, LeBoeuf and Bogle.
   b. Physician's Guide to Investing by Doroghazi and French
   c. Four Pillars of Investing by Bernstein

Chapter 21
Checklist for Resident Personal Finance

1. **Automate your Financial Life**
    - ☐ If there is a way to put a bill on auto-pay or auto draft, do it.

2. **Build Your Budgets**
    "Earn like a resident, live like a medical student."
    - ☐ Monthly
    - ☐ Annual

3. **Build your Emergency Fund**
    - ☐ Plan to get at least one month of living expenses in a bank account.
    - ☐ Work towards a 6 month emergency fund.

4. **Insurance**
    - ☐ Review your health insurance.
    - ☐ Apply for personal disability insurance (as much as your budget can allow).
    - ☐ Obtain life insurance if others depend on your income.

5. **Taxes**
    - ☐ Learn how to do your own taxes.
    - ☐ Start learning ways to minimize your taxes through itemized deductions.

6. **Maximize your Education Fund**
    - ☐ Determine the rules of use
    - ☐ Spend your education fund wisely

7. **Long Range Planning**
    - ☐ USMLE / COMLEX Step 3
    - ☐ Medical License / DEA / DPS numbers
    - ☐ Savings for Board Certification Exams

8. **Determine how to treat your Medical School Loans**
    - ☐ Collect all the information on your medical school loans
    - ☐ Make a decision on IBR vs. postponing your loan repayment.

9. **Resident Retirement Savings**
    - ☐ Start your retirement savings today.
    - ☐ Take advantage of the employer match, if possible.

Chapter 22
The Basics of Resident Moonlighting

Seen as a rite of passage for some and a way to make some extra money for others, moonlighting is a way to make some extra money while going through your residency training.

Moonlighting is one of the most contentious aspects of resident life with regards to residents and residency programs.

There are multiple aspects of moonlighting that need to be managed to be successful.

1. **Financial Impacts of Moonlighting**
   a. Moonlighting is a way to make extra income at a second job, while not neglecting your first job . . . your residency.
   b. Financial concerns is perhaps the number one reason residents moonlight.
   c. As a resident moonlighting, you can bring in a significantly higher hourly rate
      i. $50/hour is not uncommon

2. **Logistics of Moonlighting**
   a. **Approval**
      i. Before starting to moonlight, you need to receive approval from your home residency department and institution.
      ii. If you moonlight without approval, <u>you can get fired from your residency.</u>

   b. **Time**
      i. When moonlighting during an ACGME approved residency, the hours moonlighting are included within the 80 hour work week.

   c. **Location**
      i. Moonlighting can be internal (within the same institution as your residency) or external (at another institution).

   ii. **Internal Moonlighting**
      1. Can be the best type of moonlighting
      2. This allows you to use your training institution's medical malpractice insurance to cover you.
      3. This also allows you to be in close contact with faculty members, so that you have a "back-up" should you get into trouble.
      4. Internal moonlighting potentially has the least amount of start up costs related to medical licensure, medical malpractice, and other related costs.
         a. You may be able to moonlight using your PIT license.

      b.   If not, you will need to obtain your Full Medical License, DEA, and DPS numbers.

iii. External moonlighting

1. Can be a good growing experience
2. Can give you a chance to work for a group you may want to join when you graduate
3. Usually, you will need to spend money to earn money.
   a. You can have expensive start up costs.
      i. Medical licensure and DEA/DPS numbers
      ii. You will need these things to work after graduation, so these costs will be incurred during residency anyway.
   b. Medical Malpractice Insurance
      i. See complete discussion below.
      ii. If you are doing external moonlighting, your residency medical malpractice insurance will not cover you.

d. Medical Malpractice Insurance

i. The Basics

1. Medical malpractice insurance covers you professionally, should someone sue you while you are working.
2. There are two types of coverage:

   a. Occurrence Polices
   i. These polices cover only those lawsuits that occur while you are working at the company.
   ii. If you leave the company, then the lawsuits are filed, you do not have coverage.
      1. On most lawsuits, complainants have up to 2 years to file a lawsuit after it occurs.
      2. For lawsuits involving minors, it can be filed up until they turn 18 or 21 years old, depending on the state.

   b. Claims Made Polices with Tail Coverage
   i. These polices cover you for every patient you see when you are working there, even if you are sued after you leave the company.
   ii. Tail coverage is an insurance policy to cover you after you leave the company.

    ii. **Purchasing Malpractice Insurance**
1. One of the potential deal breakers for moonlighting, because of the expense.
2. Find out if you need to obtain your own medical malpractice insurance, or if the company provides it.
   a. If the company provides it, you must get Claims Made Polices with tail coverage.
   b. If they only offer an Occurrence policy, then buy your own insurance.
      i. It would be really unfortunate if you saw a patient as a resident, and they waited to file the lawsuit until you were staff.
      ii. Make sure to get your malpractice insurance agreement in writing.

3. **The Benefits of Moonlighting**
   a. In most residency programs, you will be earning about $50k-$60k per year.
      i. This is good money and, depending on the part of the country you are going to live in, you can live quite well.
   b. Some residents will choose to moonlight to help:
      i. Pay extra bills
      ii. Support a family
      iii. Pay back student loans
      iv. Provide child care
      v. Get experience in the "real world"

4. **The Challenges of Moonlighting**
   a. **Residency Restrictions**
      i. Your residency program has an obligation to ensure that you are well trained during your time.
      ii. Some residency programs have stipulations on which residents may/may not moonlight.
         1. These restrictions may depend on academic or clinical performance.
      iii. Always get approval from your department/institution before moonlighting.
         1. As stated above, it could be a potentially residency ending move.

b. **ACGME work duty hour restrictions**
    i.   Residents can only work 80 hours each week and must have 1 day off every 7 days, averaged over 4 weeks.
    ii. Great system to prevent burnout, but it makes it harder to moonlight since moonlighting hours (both internal and external) count toward the work hour restrictions.
    iii. Keep accurate records of your moonlighting to help prove you are not violating work duty hours.

c. **Work / Life Balance**
    i.   Your first priority during residency is to your training program and your family.
    ii. Even without moonlighting, balancing residency and home life is difficult.
    iii. In addition to work duty hours, you will need time to:
        1. study for your board certification
        2. study for specialty specific exams during training, and
        3. spend time with friends and family.
    iv. Trying to moonlight can be dangerous to your training and your mental health.
    v. However, moonlighting can be done safely. You may need to pick wisely the rotations during which you will moonlight, because some will be more time intensive than others.
        1. Do not over commit. Your training is a marathon, not a sprint.

Chapter 23
The Business of Resident Moonlighting

When you moonlight, you will either be an independent contractor (most common) or an employee of the business.

To moonlight successfully, you will need to actively manage your moonlighting like a small business. This will be good practice for those of you interested in running your own practice.

1. **Spending Money to Make Money**
   a. In most situations, you will have to spend money to start your moonlighting.
   b. You will need to pay the following expenses before moonlighting:
      i. State Medical License
         1. Before the end of your residency/fellowship, you will need to purchase your unrestricted medical license.
         2. Since this expense must occur during residency, why not try and make back some of the cost of the license.
      ii. DEA / DPS Numbers

2. **Medical Malpractice Insurance**
   a. Possibly needed for internal moonlighting
   b. Absolutely needed for external moonlighting
   c. Get several quotes from medical malpractice companies to figure out how many shifts a month you will have to work to pay for the insurance.
      i. The insurance may be too expensive to purchase unless you are putting in several shifts a month moonlighting.

3. **The Basics of Moonlighting Taxes**
   I could write volumes on the minutia of taxes, but in the interest of keeping this discussion brief, I'll stick to the very basics.

   a. **Background**
      i. When you moonlight, you will be earning money that may/may not have income taxes taken out of it before you receive the money.
         1. For **internal moonlighting,** taxes will more than likely be taken out before you receive the paycheck.
         2. For **external moonlighting,** taxes may/may not be removed.
            a. You may be asked to fill out a W4 that will request how much money to be withheld.
            b. Even if taxes are removed, there may not be enough taxes removed to fully pay your tax bill.
            c. Find out before you start moonlighting if taxes are removed or not, so that you can plan accordingly.

b. **Income and Self-Employment Taxes**
   i. Self-Employment Taxes are calculated based on your moonlighting income minus expenses required to moonlight.
   ii. Tracking moonlighting related expenses will help decrease your taxes and improve your income.

c. **Moonlighting Tax Deductions**
   i. Maximize your income by being tax wise with your moonlighting money.
   ii. The key to tax deductions is that they must be costs incurred while doing the moonlighting, or things you need to moonlight, and are not being used for other purposes.
      1. **Brief Example:**
         a. Medical Malpractice used for moonlighting is tax deductible, because you only use it for moonlighting.
         b. A computer that you use for personal use and for record keeping is not tax deductible.

d. **Common Resident Moonlighting Deductions**
   i. Your **work uniform**, if not used at your residency job.
   ii. **Record keeping software**, if used only for your moonlighting job.
   iii. Because your home is your "office", the commute from your home to your moonlighting job may be tax deductible (mileage for your car or bus/subway passes used for the commute only)

e. **Costs that probably won't be deducted:**
   i. The following is a list of things that **can't be deducted from your moonlighting income**:
      1. **Medical License and DEA/DPS numbers:** these are usually not deductible because residents need this to be in a residency program, not just for moonlighting.
      2. Any equipment you use for the moonlighting business and for other purposes, such as **stethoscopes, medical books, and scrubs** used for both moonlighting and residency purposes.

f. **Spending Caveat**
   i. Be cautious when spending money on your moonlighting business expenses for the "tax write off". People tend to over spend for their home based business because they can get a tax write off. (See "The Tax Deduction" box towards the end of this chapter.)
   ii. **For example:** Do you really need a new computer to run your moonlighting business?
      1. To be used as a write off, the equipment, service, etc. must be used only for the business.

2. For most resident physicians, trying to write off a home office for moonlighting probably isn't worth the hassle.
    a. But if you are interested, by all means check out the home office write off and use it at your own peril.
3. Review *Publication 587 from IRS.GOV for full details*.
    iii. Only spend money on what you absolutely need when starting to moonlight.
        1. Once you start making an income, you can purchase other things to make the job more enjoyable.

Example of using a Tax Deduction as an excuse to spend money:

Resident Rena bought a laptop for her moonlighting business. She is in the 25% tax bracket and spent $1000 on the computer, so she could reduce the amount of her taxes.

Because a tax deduction is treated by the IRS as if she never earned the money in the first place, she does not have to pay taxes on that amount.

The Math:
Her deduction is calculated as the following:
$1,000 x 0.25 = $250
So Resident Rena will not have to pay $250 in federal taxes which is great. However, she spent $1,000 so she didn't have to pay $250.

If she needed the computer for her moonlighting business, then it was a great deal. If she really didn't need it, it was a bad deal.

Bottom Line: Don't spend money just to get a tax deduction.

---

4. **Filing Your Taxes**
    a. I recommend filing your own taxes for several reasons:
        i. You learn how much you pay in taxes each year.
        ii. You learn how tax deductions affect your tax burden.
        iii. You understand how your taxes are calculated, so it helps you become more tax savvy.
    b. I have used TurboTax (~ $45) for years. You can use any program you want, or you can use the PDFs from the IRS website: www.IRS.gov.
    c. **Spend money wisely where it will save you time and headaches.**
        i. When you fill out your taxes using the computer, it will automatically fill out the correct forms so that you pay the income tax and self employment tax (along with the tax deduction for paying self employment taxes).
        ii. It will have you fill out a 1040, a schedule C (small business), and possibly a Schedule SE (self employment taxes) when you moonlight.

5. **Paying Quarterly Taxes**
   a. **Background:**
      i. If you do external moonlighting, you will receive a paycheck from your residency and another paycheck from your moonlighting gig. Both places of employment have no idea how much money is being withheld for federal and state income taxes.
      ii. Thus it is up to you to pay estimated taxes on the earnings from the moonlighting gig so that there won't be taxes and penalties due at tax time. (If you owe more than $1,000 in taxes, you will also be charged interest and penalties.)
   b. To avoid getting a tax bill, you should be paying estimated taxes on the earnings of the moonlighting gig every quarter (every 3 months).
      i. To estimate your taxes from your moonlighting:
         1. Add all your income every three months from your moonlighting job.
         2. Subtract all the moonlighting related expenses for those months.
         3. These two steps give you your net income for that quarter.
         4. Multiply your net income by your top tax bracket (usually 25% for single residents).
         5. Send this money to the IRS using the 1040-ES form.

Quarterly Taxes Example:

Resident Rena is a single resident, who earns $50k annually from her residency. She started moonlighting in January of this year and earned $2k/month moonlighting in Jan and Feb and earned $2,500 in March. She is able to walk to the moonlighting gig, and pays $350/month in medical malpractice.

Resident Rena's Moonlighting

	Income	Medical Malpractice	Net income
January	$2,000	-$350	$1,650
February	$2,000	-$350	$1,650
March	$2,500	-$350	$2,150
1st Quarter Income			$5,450

Because Resident Rena earned $5,450 after expenses, she uses this amount to calculate her taxes. She is in the 25% tax bracket and calculates her estimated taxes: $5,450 x 0.25 = $1,362.50.

Resident Rena decides to send $1,360 to the IRS by April 15th. (Good thing she stashed away money from each paycheck.)

Chapter 24
Resident Moonlighting Checklist

1. **Logistics of Moonlighting**
   a. Keep your residency happy
      - ☐ Obtain approval from your department
      - ☐ Will your duty hours allow you to moonlight?
         - ☐ How many hours do you expect to work?
   b. Location
      - ☐ Internal moonlighting
      - ☐ External moonlighting
   c. Keep your family happy
      - ☐ Is the time away from your family to earn the extra money worth it?

2. **Business of Moonlighting**
   a. **Costs**:
      - ☐ Medical license
      - ☐ DEA number
      - ☐ DPS state number
      - ☐ +/- Medical Malpractice (depends on moonlighting job)
         - ☐ Calculate the costs to see if it is even worth the time and money to moonlight.
         - ☐ How much will you have to work to pay for the medical malpractice insurance?
         - • If you need to purchase your own medical practice, obtain Claims Made with tail coverage
   b. **Taxes and Moonlighting:**
      - ☐ Keep track of expenses and income from your moonlighting.
      - ☐ File your quarterly estimated taxes so you don't pay back taxes and penalties.
         - ☐ Keep track of the estimated taxes paid, so that you can record this on your federal tax return.
      - • Forms at www.IRS.gov
         - ☐ Publication 587 - home office deduction
         - ☐ Schedule C - itemized deductions
         - ☐ Schedule ES - estimated quarterly taxes

Chapter 25
The Financial Transition Between Residency and Fellowship/Staff

Once you have the job and your credentials, you will be going through another life transition.

1. **Credentialing**
   a. This is the process by which your group or hospital makes sure you have the proper training to do the job you were hired to do.
   b. All of your training, requested privileges, and letters of recommendation are all put under a microscope.
   c. This process can **take 6 to 8 months to complete.**
      i. Have a plan in place for covering yourself for the next several months if your credentialing takes longer than you anticipated.
2. **Potential Loss of Income During Your Transition.**
   a. You should know during your contract negotiations when you will receive your first paycheck.
   b. Depending on the type of practice you join, it may be 3 months until you receive your first paycheck after you start working.
   c. You may also need time between jobs for moving, taking boards, travel, or relaxation.
      i. It's not a bad idea to have some down time, but make sure you have a plan for paying the bills when you are in between jobs.
3. **Funding the Transition**
   a. You have been earning an income for at least the last three years . . . and you know this transition is coming, so prepare for it by saving.
   b. A less than stellar way to fund this is through credit cards or loans.
4. **Beware the "Loaning Group"**
   Be cautious of groups that want to loan you money when you are starting.
   I call these groups "Loaning Groups".
   a. **The Set Up**
      i. You are given a loan as "salary" for the first three years so you can get your feet on the ground and establish your own billing.
      ii. After three years, for each year you remain with the group, a year of the loan is forgiven. (*See the example on the next page.*)
   b. **The Problem**
      i. This seems like a good deal . . . until you file your taxes.
      ii. Loan forgiveness from a non-government business is considered a taxable event by the IRS.

"Loaning Group" example:

Faulty Bob is a new cardiologist who joined an existing group. He signed a contract with the group that provides him a guaranteed salary of $180k annually for three years as a loan. (This provides a salary for him while he builds up his patient base.) If he stays with the group, then the loan is forgiven for each year he continues to work for the group.

This sounds like a great deal until tax time.

Because Dr. Bob's income for the first three years were loans:
1. He was not able to put money into retirement savings.
   1. (You need an earned income to contribute to any retirement account)
2. He did not pay any taxes on the "income", which he would have used to live on.
   1. However, when the $ 180,000 in loans are "discharged" each year, the IRS views this as "income". (See table below)
3. Dr. Bob now owes $ 44,297, plus the loan forgiveness taxes ($59,400) and this also pushed him into the 2nd to highest tax bracket.

	Loan from his group	Salary from his group	Federal Taxes paid on loan	Federal Taxes Paid	Total Tax Burden
Year 1	$ 180,000	$0	$0	$0	$0
Year 2	$ 180,000	$0	$0	$0	$0
Year 3	$ 180,000	$0	$0	$0	$0
Year 4	$0	$ 180,000	$ 59,400	$ 44,297	$ 103,697
Year 5	$0	$ 180,000	$ 59,400	$ 44,297	$ 103,697
Year 6	$0	$ 180,000	$ 59,400	$ 44,297	$ 103,697

5. **Health Insurance Coverage**
   a. Don't go without health insurance coverage.
   b. Obtain an extension of your current health insurance.
      i. Also called "COBRA" which stands for Consolidated Omnibus Budget Reconciliation Act.
      ii. Review your current coverage to find out if you have a grace period after ending your resident health insurance, that would allow you to retroactively pay if you had a health problem.
   c. See if you can get your new health insurance to start before you start your new job.
      i. Not likely, but worth asking

6. **Plan for Moving Expenses**
   a. Deposits for
      i. New apartment
      ii. Telephone
      iii. Cable service
      iv. Utilities
   b. Moving your belongings
      i. Maintain good records of your move.
      ii. Some groups may reimburse you for your moving expenses.
      iii. You may be able to get a tax write off if you are moving more than 50 miles for your job.

7. **Keep Track of Benefits From Your Residency**
   a. Some residents are employees of hospitals or government entities.
      i. Some entities are set up to reward time spent in the system.
      ii. Be sure to get a summary of the time spent in that system, so that if you return to the system, you have accrued that time.
      iii. Example:
         1. You work as a resident for 5 years for a state university.
         2. You graduate and go to work for a private group, then return in 3 years to the state university system.
         3. When you return, the state system gives you 5 years of service and may potentially give you back your unused sick leave.
            a. This is important when advancement, retirement, and vacation time may be determined by years of service.

8. **Roll Over Your Retirement Account**
   a. Have your resident employer rollover your resident retirement account.
   b. You can either put it in your new retirement account, or roll it over to a rollover IRA.
      i. Most personal finance gurus recommend a rollover IRA, because you have more investment options than a traditional retirement account.

Chapter 26
The Brief Resident to Staff Checklist

☐ **Prepare for your new job**
    ☐ Credentialing may take a while, prepare yourself for that.
        ☐ Keep on top of credentialing paperwork.
        ☐ Keep in close communication with your new group.

☐ **Plan for your potential loss of income between paychecks.**

☐ **Funding your transitions**
    ☐ **Plan to save for the move.**
    ☐ **As a last resort, use a loan or a credit card.**

☐ **Beware of the Loaning group.**

☐ **Maintain your health insurance coverage.**

☐ **Obtain all your information related to your resident employment.**

☐ **Roll over your resident retirement to a rollover IRA.**

Part Three: The Young Staff Years

Chapter 27
Philosophy of Young Staff Personal Finance

"85% of lottery winners are bankrupt within 5 years of receiving the prize money."

-Dave Ramsey
author: *The Total Money Makeover*

"As a result, no matter how much someone earns, expenses tend to match income. This is called lifestyle inflation."

-Jacob Lund Fisker
author: *Early Retirement Extreme*

1. Introduction

The **first financial shock** I got as a new staff was my first paycheck as a pediatric anesthesiologist. It was the largest paycheck I had ever seen in my life.

The **second financial shock** I got was when one of my senior partners asked me to contribute to the staff Christmas Party . . . which was more than my family's entire Christmas budget!

Welcome to the world of a staff physician.

There are financial parts of being a staff physician that few people talk about, because it is taboo. I am going to discuss those things in this chapter.

2. The (Physician) Millionaire Next Door

The Millionaire Next Door is a must read classic book by Thomas J. Stanley and William D. Danko.

One group of high end earners that they focused on was physicians. The authors go on to describe those things that separates the wealthy physicians from the un-wealthy physicians.

> "Our research has found that physicians in general do not tend to be wealth accumulators"
>
> "...among all major high-income-producing occupations, physicians have a significantly low propensity to accumulate substantial wealth"
>
> -The Millionaire Next Door by Stanley & Danko

a. Within the book, the authors found **six reasons why physicians don't build wealth**:
    1. There is an inverse relationship between education and wealth.
    2. The "Doctor Status" (what you drive, where you live, and what you spend) that which society expects from physicians.
    3. Generally physicians contribute a higher percentage of income to charities.
    4. Physicians are less likely to receive inheritance from parents than other siblings.
    5. Physicians are asked by parents to take care of less well off brothers and sisters.
    6. Physicians tend to neglect their financial well-being, because of the amount of time they spend on their career day to day.

3. **Financial Anchoring**
    a. Anchoring is the economic term for when you start paying a particular price for something and expect it to be "normal".
        i. For example: $4 dollars for a cup of coffee seems quite normal, when just a few years ago, it would have been seen as outrageous in light of the $0.25 bottomless cup of coffee.

4. **Beware of Young Staff Physician Anchoring**
    a. It will be very easy to spend lots of money because your view of what is expensive will change . . . as in my example of the Christmas party collection.
    b. When you become a staff physician, what at first seems expensive, will change into "not that expensive" because:
        i. If you are like most physicians, your income will increase dramatically.
        ii. You will see the cars your partners drive, the homes they own, and the trips they go on and it is tempting to want that same lifestyle.
    c. **This is keeping up with "the Dr. Jones" and it can lead to financial devastation and is a non-winning game.**
        i. Expectations of what kind of car, house, vacations, and lifestyle you should have can cause you to burn through even a large paycheck.
    d. **You will be tempted to grow into that lifestyle even though:**
        i. You have larger medical school debt loads than they did.
        ii. Your partners have been out practicing longer.
        iii. Your salary will be lower starting in the practice.

5. **Budget, Plan and Prepare**
   a. If you want that nice car, save up for it.
   b. If you want that house, save for the 20% down payment.
   c. You decide how you spend your money, however, keep in mind the long term goals that you also want to achieve.

6. **Beware of "Financial Advisors"**
   a. Not all "advisors" are required to look out for your financial well being.
      i. This is called a fiduciary responsibility and not all financial advisors are held to this standard.
      ii. Just because an investment is complicated, doesn't necessarily mean that it will provide a good return.
         1. Do not invest in anything that you can not explain to someone else.

7. **Expect to be asked for donations.**
   a. Be prepared that you will be asked by different people to donate money, because now you are a "real" doctor.
   b. When you do donate, and I think you should, work it into your budget, and make sure that it is in line with your values.
      i. In light of *The Millionaire Next Door*, budget your giving and balance it with your other obligations such as your medical school debt repayment, your children's' college savings, and taking care of your aging parents.

8. **Resources**
   a. The Millionaire Next Door by Thomas J. Stanley and William D. Danko
   b. The Physician's Guide to Investing by Robert M. Doroghazi

Chapter 28
Basic Young Staff Finance

The best financial advice I got from a faculty physician, when I was a resident, was "Keep your life simple". The main difference between your financial life as a resident and a staff physician, is size and scale. The basic principals of personal finance still remain the same.

1. **Earn like a Staff, Live like a Resident.**
   For the first few years, maintain your lifestyle similar to how you lived as a resident. Stay in this mindset, at least for your first few years as staff, and it will put you way ahead.
   a. **Staff Budget:**
      i. It will be very easy to blow through huge amounts of money without realizing it.
      ii. Budgeting as a young faculty is similar to budgeting as a resident, but the size and scale are increased.
         1. Plan where your money goes before you spend it, because it is very easy to spend much more money that you think possible.
      iii. Expand some parts of your budget (eating out, fun money, etc) but keep it in check.
         1. Giving your family some breathing room by increasing your eating out fund, spending more fun money, etc. will allow you to enjoy your new salary, but will help keep you from blowing through the whole paycheck.
   b. **Rework your Monthly and Annual Budget**
      i. As you did when you where a resident, figure out your take home pay and rework your new budgets.
      ii. Most of you will have to budget for an increased student loan payment.
      iii. Most professional organizations cost more when you complete residency/fellowship, so budget accordingly.
2. **Personal Emergency Fund for Young Staff**
   a. **Most financial advisors recommend saving 3-6 months of expenses.**
      i. I recommend **at least 6 months of expenses in a savings account plus at least another 3 to 6 months of expenses** in an account that can be accessed in 6 months.
      ii. You should have a total of **9 to 12 months of expenses** saved up for emergencies.

b. **Why such a large emergency fund?**
   i. It takes longer for a physician to find a new job than for a less specialized professional.
      1. The more specialized you become, the more difficult it will be to find another job, or one that pays as much as your current one.
      2. Credentialing at hospitals can take up to 6 months to happen.
   ii. A job change could also mean moving to a new location because of the job, or because of a **non-compete clause.**
      1. A **non-compete clause** is part of most physician contracts. Should you leave a group, you can not legally work within a certain geographical range (typically 30 to 50 miles).
      2. The point of a non-compete clause is to keep physicians from "stealing" business if they leave a group.
   iii. You may also have to leave the geographic area, because it is saturated with the same specialists.

c. **"I'm a physician, why would I ever need to look for a new job?"**
   i. Barring egregious negligence, substance abuse, or major personality issues, your career is solid in medicine. Your job, however, is not.
   ii. Any number of things can happen
      1. within your group or department:
         a. You get a new Chief or Chair that brings his/her own people in and you are replaced.
      2. external to your group:
         a. Your group loses the contract with the hospital where you work.

3. **Medical Malpractice Insurance Emergency Fund**
   a. Depending on your coverage and your contract, you may need to pay your own tail coverage for your medical malpractice insurance.
      i. Tail coverage extends medical malpractice insurance after you leave a group through job change or retirement.
   b. If you are in this situation, understand how much tail coverage you will need to pay so that this can be included on top of your emergency fund.
      i. For some specialties, this can be more than $30k, paid by you, as a lump sum payment.
   c. This "Tail Coverage" emergency fund is the ultimate parachute to extract you from a bad group/situation and allows you to transition to a better group.

4. **Health Insurance**
    a. Check with your group to make sure your health insurance is in place.
    b. Talk with your partners to find good physicians in your area to go to.
5. **Disability Insurance for the Young Staff**
    a. Your biggest asset is your ability to earn a living.
    b. If you have not set up your disability insurance, **do it now.**
    c. Your new job may have group disability insurance.
        i. If so, set up personal disability insurance first, then set up your disability insurance through your employer.
            1. You may be limited in how much personal insurance you can purchase on your own once your group insurance is in place.
            2. Group disability insurance is cheaper, but has more limitations.
            3. Private disability insurance can be carried with you to a new employer.
    d. It is vital that you develop your new staff budget during the time you are buying this insurance, so that you know how much benefit you would need each month to pay your basic bills.
    e. Check periodically to see if you should increase your disability insurance, if you already have it.
        i. With every increase in pay, you may want to increase your insurance coverage.
        ii. Disability insurance is supposed to cover up to 60% of your salary, should you be unable to work.
            1. Some physicians, however, will not be able to obtain a large enough policy to cover 60% of their salary, because they have such a large income.
            2. Increasing your coverage as your income increases helps keep you on top of this issue.
6. **Life Insurance for the Young Staff**
    a. If other people depend on your income (spouse, children, parents, etc.) it is vital that you start your life insurance with Term Life insurance.
        i. This is the cheapest life insurance to purchase, and can be a real lifesaver if something happens to you before you are well established.
    b. If you don't have this in place, do it now.
7. **Auto Insurance**
    a. Increase your deductible once you have your emergency fund in place
    b. Increase your coverage as well.
        i. Because of your new increased income, you will have a larger target on your back should you or your family become involved in a auto collision.

8. **Homeowners/Renters Insurance**
   a. Increase your coverage for theft and liability.
   b. Obtain an umbrella policy to cover liability over all your assets.
      i. If someone comes into your home, falls through the ceiling, and is injured, you will want the coverage.

9. **Retirement Savings for Young Faculty**
   a. If you have not started saving for retirement, do it now.
   b. You should have a good plan in place before starting to save for your children's college or any other long term savings.
   c. See *Chapter 29* for a full discussion.

10. **Start Saving for your Children's College Fund**
   a. After you have your budget established to cover your expenses, including debt repayment, and retirement, you need to start saving for your children's higher education.
      i. Review *Chapters 9 and 10* earlier in this book on how to save for your children's higher education.
      ii. More than likely, you will be earning too much to qualify for government grants and loans.

I know too many physicians who plan to cash-flow their children's college expenses.

This might have worked for your senior partners, however, in the current climate of decreasing physician reimbursement and increasing college expenses, it is a bad idea.

If you want to pay off your own debt first, then focus on saving for your children's college, that is fine . . . just have a plan for how you are going to fund your children's education if that is something you want to do.

---

11. **Start Planning Financial Support for your Parents**
    a. Many young faculty will find themselves in the position of needing to help support their aging parents.
    b. This can occur in several forms including:
        i.   Helping to pay off your student loan debt that they took out for you.
        ii. Helping to pay your parents' current bills.
        iii. Helping to pay Long Term Care insurance.
            1. Review *Chapter 3, Long Term Care Insurance*
            2. Long Term Care Insurance is some of the most expensive insurance you can purchase.
                i. This insurance will likely be more expensive than your disability insurance.
            3. When/if your parents need this care, they can use a private nursing home.
            4. This insurance gives you and your family options that are not available through Medicare.

12. **Attack Credit Card Debt and Other Loans.**
    a. I recommend the Loan Size Plan.
    b. Come up with a plan for all your debt on:
        i.   credit cards
        ii. relocation loans
        iii. other high interest loans.
    c. Review *Chapter 6* and get to it.

Chapter 29
Medical School Loan Debt Treatment for the Young Staff

Whether you have been paying on your school loans as a resident through IBR or you have yet to start, your time to start paying on these loans have some due.

1. **Review Your Loan Information**
   a. If you haven't already, learn all companies that have your loans.
   b. Learn the new payment schedule related to your income.
   c. If you have been doing IBR, and expect to utilize the Loan Forgiveness program, then make sure all the paperwork is in place.

2. **Start Paying off Your School Loans.**
   a. All loans bring some risk with them, some are more risky (higher interest rates) than others.
   b. If you have been paying on your loans through IBR and are in a situation to take advantage of the Loan Forgiveness program, then pay on schedule.
      i. The advantage of having significant amounts of your loans forgiven is worth keeping the loan through the end of the ten years.
   c. If you are not able to utilize the Loan Forgiveness program, then consider paying off the loans to get rid of the financial burden of monthly payments.
      i. I know people will fight me on this and say that they can earn more money investing the money than the interest rate of the loan and therefore come out ahead.
      ii. This scenario was more likely when school loans had interest rates of 1-2% and the stock market was yielding 10-12% consistently.
      iii. If you want to do that, it is up to you, but you need to know the risk/benefit ratio.
   d. **Before you dismiss paying off your loans early, consider the following.**
      i. Most physicians will earn an income that will not allow them to deduct the interest on the student loans from their taxes.
      ii. People say they can earn more in the stock market than what it is costing them on their loans.
         1. Most new faculty have loans that are in the 6% range.
            a. On your investment, you would have to earn at least 6% (plus the transaction costs, and income taxes) to even break even.
            b. This makes it difficult to come out ahead.

e. Student loans are forgiven if you die (many physicians like to tell me this). However:
   i. A 30 year old is 4 times as likely to be disabled than die.
      1. If you are disabled, and can't work in your medical specialty, you will still have to pay off the loans.
      2. You are more likely to be just "disabled enough" to not practice as a physician, than you are to be completely disabled.
      3. Most student loans are not able to be discharged through bankruptcy.
         a. If you are financially devastated through a disability, you still have to pay on the loans.
         b. Trying to service your loans and your regular living expenses during your disability can lead to disaster.

f. **When you pay off your loans, you will not believe the weight that will be lifted from your shoulders.**
   i. Residents with larger debt loads have higher burn out rates, so debt brings with it a stress that is easily overlooked.
   ii. I would think that there would be very few people who would regret paying off their loans early.
   iii. Along with a home mortgage, student loan payments can decrease your monthly cash flow and increases the time till you can work part time, or retire.

Chapter 30
Home Ownership for the New Staff Physician

The most expensive purchase most people make is their home. For physicians, it is either their home, or their education. Follow the next few recommendations and you will be well on your way to avoiding some common pitfalls.

1. **Consider Renting Your First Few Years as Staff.**
   a. There are **several reasons** why I suggest this:
      i. This gives you a chance to **learn the geography** of the new area.
         1. For most physicians, there are three home qualities that are desirable:
            a. A home close to work.
            b. A home within a reasonable budget for the stage of life they are in.
            c. A home in a good school district.
         2. It is very difficult, in most home markets, to find all three in the same home.
            a. Maybe the home is close to work and affordable, but you will have to send your kids to private school because the school district is not too good.
            b. Maybe the home is affordable and in a good school district, but the drive is 30 minutes away from work.
         3. You will have to decide what the best combination for you and your family is going to be.
      ii. It gives you a chance to **learn about the group, the town, and other opportunities**.
      iii. There are a handful of new faculty who **only stay at their new job for a year or two** before changing jobs.
      iv. The first job **may not reach expectations of pay, work load, or location**.
      v. This gives you a chance to start **paying down on your school loans**.
      vi. This gives you the opportunity to leave an area **without being saddled with an asset that may be difficult to sell: a house.**
      vii. This also gives you the chance to build up a **down payment for your home**.
      viii. It also gives you the <u>chance to focus on your new career</u>.
         1. You will want as few distractions as possible.
         2. Your reputation will be made or broken within the first 6 - 12 months that you are a new staff.
         3. Don't let the distraction of home ownership derail all the hard work you have put into your career.

2. **Home Purchase Considerations**
   a. Review *Chapter 5*, about the basics of home ownership.
   b. It will be very tempting to buy the largest home you can.
      i. Buy conservatively, because it is quite likely that with all the changes in healthcare, physician salaries will decrease.
         1. I personally already know physician groups that are making much less than they did several years ago. Some senior partners are earning almost half of what they were a few years ago.
   c. Some of the size of homes that your partners have will be out of your financial reach.
      1. This is keeping up with the Dr. Jones.
      2. Currently, if you want to take out a jumbo loan (>$417k), you need four separate lines of credit.

3. **Dr. Morgan's Rules of Thumb for Homes for Dentists and Physicians**
   a. Your home shouldn't be worth more than twice your annual income.
      i. Mortgage lenders will tell you can afford a much larger house; don't do it.
      ii. **For Example**: If you earn $200k, your house shouldn't be more than $400k.
   b. It will cost you **5-10% of the worth of the home annually to maintain the home**.
      i. This takes into account the mortgage, taxes, upkeep and utilities.
      ii. **Example:** A $400k home will cost about $20k to $40k each year.
   c. **Dr. Morgan's Rules Application**
      i. When you are considering buying a home that is larger than you need, realize that you are potentially setting yourself up with some heavy costs to maintain it.
      ii. Although some physicians buy the $1million home, they are still having to pay $100k to $200k each year to maintain the home.
      iii. When you are thinking about buying a second home, its not only the cost of the home, but the annual expenses that can really add up.

4. **Consider Paying Off Your Home Early**
   a. Paying off your home early will free up monthly money that can be used elsewhere.
   b. One of the determinants of being able to retire is a home that is paid for.
   c. Even though some say money can be invested in other things, and earn more than paying off your home, those that pay off their home never regret it.
      i. If you pay off your home, and don't like it, then you can remortgage your home and get a house payment again.

5. **Review Chapter 33 regarding Asset Protection and Your Home**
   a. Make your own decision about utilizing your home in an asset protection plan.

Chapter 29
Staff Physician Retirement Planning

Hopefully you have been saving for retirement during your residency/ fellowship training. If not, then this is the time to put the retirement engine into overdrive.

Please refer to the basics of retirement savings in Chapter 11, and then forge ahead.

1. **Roll Over all your Retirement Plans**
   As you work throughout your career, you may collect retirement accounts at different companies, in different plans, and in different types of investments.
   a. By rolling these over to a rollover IRA, you will have control over your retirement savings.
   b. The key is to have the money in the retirement account go directly to the company with whom you are having the Rollover Account established.
   c. If you have the retirement account cashed out instead, then:
      i. You lose that money growing tax free.
      ii. You will have to pay a penalty.
      iii. You will have to pay income taxes on the account.
   d. This is the time to organize your retirement accounts so that you know:
      i. How much you have.
      ii. What it is invested in.
      iii. What company holds the retirement account.

2. **Review Your Options with Your Employer.**
   a. You may have a combination of 401k/403b and 457 or pension plans.
      i. Review *Chapter 11* for the various aspects of these accounts.
   b. These retirement plans usually have a financial advisor who works for the investment company, that can get you started investing.
   c. Max out all your retirement accounts when you start working.
      i. Because your income will be larger than your salary as a resident/fellow, you will never "miss" the money.
      ii. Find out if a company match is available.

3. **What other retirement options are available?**
   a. If your company does not provide a retirement plan, then **start a SEP-IRA and use it.**
   b. Roth IRAs are typically unavailable for higher income earners.
   c. However, high income earners may be able to place money in a Traditional IRA:
      i. It will not be tax deductible.
      ii. Growth is tax free.
      iii. You have to track your basis (the principle amount you put into the account), so you don't have taxes on this amount.
   d. There is also the Roth "work around".
      i. You place money into a traditional IRA.
         1. Because you earn too much, you can not deduct it.
      ii. You then convert the traditional IRA to a Roth IRA.
         1. As of 2013, there is no income limit restricting the conversion of traditional IRAs to Roth IRAs.
         2. Taxes will be due on any funds that were paid into the account with pre-tax money.
         3. Because you already paid taxes on the money, no extra tax money will be due when you withdraw it.

4. **Other Savings in Non-Retirement Accounts**
   a. Once you have maxed out the total amount you can save in retirement accounts, and want to save more, then turn towards regularly taxed accounts:
      i. Savings accounts
      ii. Money Market accounts
      iii. Investments such as stocks, mutual funds, and bonds
      iv. Real estate and investment properties
   b. By investing in these accounts, you will not be bound by stipulations of when and how you withdraw money from these accounts.

5. **How to Prepare for Retirement**
   a. Its always a good idea to start with the end in mind.
      i. This will give you focus to achieve your goals.
   b. One of the best books written on retirement is <u>Smart Couples Finish Rich</u> by David Bach.
      i. His philosophy on retirement savings is to have a vision for what you want out of retirement, set goals on how to obtain your vision, then use systematic savings and investing to get there.
      ii. I don't agree with everything he offers, but I definitely recommend this book.

6. **How Much Should you be Saving?**
   a. **Start by saving 10-20% of your take home pay.**
      i. This is the figure most financial gurus will tell you to save.
         1. 10-20% is a good place to start for most people, however, while most professionals have been working, physicians have been in training for 7 to 10 years (or longer).
            a. This puts physicians behind in saving for retirement.
      ii. Although physicians are earning a salary during residency and fellowship, few concentrate on retirement savings, because the focus has been on "study now, the money will come to you later".

   b. **Calculate How Much to Save**.
      i. Remember from *Chapter 11*, that you can use the "Back of the Envelope" to calculate how much you need to save for retirement.
      ii. When you start looking at larger salaries ($100k/year and greater), the amount "needed" for that income replacement can be staggering.
      iii. Some of these numbers are unobtainable without some serious savings.

   c. **Look at your budget and how much it takes to run your lifestyle.**
      i. You might not have enough money to retire into the lifestyle you expect.

To Replace this Annual Income	You Need This in Savings
$100,000	$2,500,000
$200,000	$5,000,000
$250,000	$6,250,000
$500,000	$12,500,000
$750,000	$18,750,000
$1,000,000	$25,000,000

      ii. While many physicians think and talk about when they will retire, they might not be able to completely decide on the timing of their retirement.
         1. Your "job" may change in ways you have no control, which causes you to retire.
            a. If you are nearing retirement, then starting over in a new job may not have the same appeal as if you were young.
            b. Much like professional sports players, you may have a limited career depending on your specialty.

7. **Where should you invest your money?**
   a. Contact the company that is managing your retirement plan to talk with someone about your options to invest your retirement money.

    b. There are many different ways to invest and this depends on
        i. Your age
        ii. Your risk tolerance
        iii. How interested you are in the minutia of investing

8. **Plan for Your Retirement Today**
You may be retiring earlier than you plan because of multiple different factors.

    a. **External Change Beyond Your Control**
        i. Your Department Chair/Devision Chief/Senior Managing Partner may change
            1. This may bring with it leadership changes, which make it intolerable to work with your group any more.
        ii. Hospitals/Groups may be sold or closed.
        iii. Contract negotiations may fail.
        iv. Physician salaries may change because of change in insurance/government reimbursement, causing your time to be much less valuable in the workplace.

    b. **Internal Change Beyond Your Control:**
        i. You may become unable to work due to injury, disability, or health problems.
        ii. You may not be able to work in a high stress environment.
        iii. You may not be able to keep a competitive edge in your skill and may need to retire.

    c. **Changes within Your Control:**
        i. You may want to:
            1. enjoy more time with your family.
            2. not deal with the management of your practice.
            3. travel, relax, sleep in, take up a new hobby, etc.

9. **Resources:**
    a. Smart Couples Finish Rich by David Bach.
    b. Your Money or Your Life: 9 Steps to Transforming your Relationship with Money Achieving Financial Independence by Vicki Robin, Joe Dominguez and Monique Tilford.
    c. The Bogleheads' Guide to Retirement Planning by Larimore, Lindauer, Ferri, Dogu, and Bogle.
    d. The Four Pillars of Investing: Lessons for Building a Winning Portfolio by William Bernstein.

Chapter 32
Managing Your Education Fund

Many groups have education funds or Professional Development Accounts (PDA) for their physicians. This is a tax free benefit that is just as significant now as it was when you were a resident.

Academic departments are known for having these accounts, however, some private groups offer them as well.

1. **Education / Travel Account**
    a. Some institutions call this a Professional Development Account (PDA).
    b. Review what you can do with this account as a staff.
        i. Even at the same institution, as staff, you may have
            1. More flexibility in how you spend your funds.
            2. More money in this fund.
    c. It is very easy to blow through this money by going to one or two conferences.
    d. Budgeting how you are going to use this money is key to getting the most out of this fund.

2. **Learn the rules of use**
    a. How much money do you get each year?
        i. Do you have to use all each year?
        ii. Does the education fund run as an academic year or as a calendar year?
        iii. If you can carry over some of the money, how much can you carry over?
    b. Enlist the assistance of your administration personnel to learn the ins/outs of the process.
        i. What paperwork is involved?
        ii. How long before the purchase/conference do you need to submit the paperwork?
        iii. Are you able to have the department/institution pay up front when you have expenses?
        iv. Do you need to pay first, then get reimbursed?
            1. If so, consider setting up an education checking account to keep a relatively small sum of money ($3k) to pay expenses, then when the reimbursement check comes in, deposit it to this account.
            2. By setting this up, all the expenses from your education fund are kept separately from your regular household account.
            3. This acts as yet another emergency fund for you should you need it.
        v. If you are reimbursed after you pay, how soon after do you need to submit the paperwork for reimbursement?

3. **Common Education Fund Uses**
   a. Medical License, DPS/DEA Numbers
   b. Professional Organization Dues
      i. Consider using your education fund to join medical specialty organizations which can reduce your cost for conferences, journals, and special events.
   c. Subscriptions to Professional Journals
   d. Continuing Medical Education (CME)
   e. Conferences
   f. Books
   g. Computer Hardware and Software

4. **Caveats for using your Education Fund.**
   a. Find out if books/computers bought with this account if they need to be returned when you separate from your department/institution.
      i. When I separate from my department (hopefully when I retire) I will be returning my iPad 1.
      ii. I know a physician that had to return not only his computer, but also all the books he purchased with his account, even though they were outdated.

5. **Use your Education Fund to Advance your Career.**
   a. Professional Skills not related to CME
      i. Because you are a physician, and have a "terminal" degree, some departments and institutions won't pay for other degrees such as a Masters of Business Administration (MBA) or Masters of Education (mEd).
         1. Find out if there are other ways to have these degrees paid for by your institution or your department.
         2. Utilize your education fund to help defray the costs of these degrees.
   b. As an aside, unlike books and computers, your department/institution can't take away an MBA, mEd, or other degrees/certifications when you leave.

Chapter 33

The World's Shortest Chapter on Asset Protection for Physicians

This subject is well beyond the scope/scale of this book . . . .

However . . . I have to address five issues:
- one you know about (your career)
- one we already talked about (your income)
- one overlooked (your marriage)
- one over emphasized (your home)
- one least talked about (your investments)

1. **Your Medical Career**
   a. Get medical malpractice insurance.
      i. <u>1:14 physicians will get sued.</u>
      ii. So many premed students, medical students, residents and physicians worry about "the big lawsuit", that they neglect the ways most physicians lose a significant amount of money . . . the other 4 issues.
      iii. Do the right thing for the patient.
      iv. Always tell the truth and be truthful with your patients.
      v. Continue to study to be a good doctor.
         1. Learn your craft.
         2. Strive to be better.
      vi. When you are not as good as you once were, know when to hang up the stethoscope and retire.
      vii. Enough said.

2. **Your Income**
   a. If you don't have term life insurance and people depend on you, get it now.
   b. If you haven't purchased disability insurance, stop reading this book and get some.
      i. Review the disability insurance sections in *Chapters 3* and *28*.

3. **Your Marriage**
   a. We all hear about "The Big Lawsuit" . . . more like we have nightmares about it. The one lawsuit worth millions of dollars that threatens to wipe out half a physician's net worth?
   b. As many times as we hear about it, it is far more likely a physician's life savings, retirement accounts and future earnings will be wiped out by something <u>much more common: divorce.</u>
   c. **The divorce rate for physicians is about 30%:**
      i. <u>4.2/14 physicians will go through a divorce.</u>
         1. Compare that to the 1/14 who get sued.
      ii. It is far more likely to lose your assets in a divorce than in the large medical malpractice lawsuit.

      iii. Along with the emotional aspects of a divorce,
- 1. You divide your assets in half
- 2. You may have to pay for two households:
  - a. Your new household
  - b. Your former spouse's household
    - i. in the form of child support and/or alimony
- 3. You must start rebuilding your financial life.

d. Your first "asset" you should protect is your marriage.
- i. While some advocate a prenuptial agreement, there are other ways to protect your marriage:
  - 1. Spend time with your spouse/family.
  - 2. Get couples counseling before a broken relationship is unrepairable.
  - 3. Remember that no job is worth your marriage.
    - a. When you retire, you will never wish you spent more time at work than with your family.
- ii. It is not unusual for physicians to neglect their family because of the "higher calling" of medicine.

e. Remember: Happy Wife, Happy Life. or Happy Spouse, Happy House.

4. Your Home

a. The most common piece of advice given to young physicians is to buy a larger house than you need to provide a "bank" to safeguard your money.
- i. This is especially true in states with homestead laws.

b. While good in theory, it has some flaws.
- i. You have 4 ways to get money out of your home, that you put there for "safe guarding".

    1. Sell your house.
- a. You will pay 6% of your home price to realtors.
- b. You will need to find a new place to live.
- c. You may not be able to sell your home as fast as you would like.

    2. Get a mortgage and/or get a 2nd mortgage.
- a. This only works if you have equity in your home.
- b. This puts you further into debt.

    3. Get a home equity line of credit.
- a. Again, this puts you into debt.

    4. Get a reverse mortgage
- a. Perhaps the worse possible option.
- b. The bank pays you a set amount of money for every month you stay in the home.

      c.   When you leave the home, the bank owns it.
          i.   No matter how much equity you have in the home or how much money you have been paid by the bank.
      d. These loans can also be associated with heavy fees.
  c. Buy the size home that you need. Larger homes mean larger costs.
      i.   Review *Morgan's Rule of Thumb in Chapter 30.*

5. Your Investments

  a. Physicians tend to think that because they are very smart in one area (medicine), they will also be very smart in other areas (investing).
      i.   You can do allot of your own investments, but you have to learn about them.
      ii. Put in the time to learn how to invest, and you can do well.
      iii. If you don't have the time, or don't want to learn, hire a professional.
          1. You wouldn't hand over a scalpel to the 1st year medical student without a lot of oversight.
          2. Hire a Flat Fee Certified Financial Planner (CFP) and don't invest in anything you can not explain to a 5th Grader.
  b. Be wary of financial advisors who tell you that it is too complicated for you to do on your own.
      i.   You leaned the Krebbs Cycle, Organic Chemistry, and have gone through multiple standardized exams . . . you can learn this on your own, if you choose to.
      ii. It's just like any other risk/benefit analysis . . . you just have to learn the structure of the environment.
  c. Physicians love to talk about how much money they made on investments, but they will fail to tell you how they lost a ton of money on others.
  d. Many times physicians lose money in "complicated" investments or business deals.
      i.   Unless you are truly financially savvy, stick with stocks, bonds, and mutual funds.

6. Resources:

  a. www.whitecoatinvestor.com - for your self education in investing.
  b. Physician's Guide to Investing by Doroghazi and French

Chapter 34
The Checklist for Young Staff Physicians

1. **Earn like a Staff, Live like a Resident.**
   - ☐ Get your finances in order to start a successful career.

2. **Build Your Budgets**
   - ☐ Monthly
   - ☐ Annual

3. **Build Your Emergency Fund**
   - ☐ Standard physician emergency fund
     - ☐ At least 6 months expenses in a high yield savings account, plus another 3 to 6 months of expenses in relatively easy to get at investments.
   - ☐ Medical malpractice tail coverage fund
     - ☐ Check your contract to see if you need to have this fund.

4. **Health Insurance**

5. **Life Insurance**
   - ☐ Get it in place if you have people depending on you and your income to survive.
   - ☐ If you already have life insurance, increase the coverage to match your new salary.

6. **Disability Insurance**
   - ☐ Protect your biggest asset: your ability to earn a living.
   - ☐ Get private insurance in place before signing up for group insurance.

7. **Housing**
   - ☐ Consider renting your first few years as being a staff physician.
   - ☐ Review *Chapters 5 and 30.*
   - ☐ Review "Dr. Morgan's Rule of Thumb" for homes.

8. **Medical School Loans**
   - ☐ Get the loans out of your life.
   - ☐ Check to see if you qualify for IBR and Public Loan Forgiveness Programs.
     - ☐ Start getting the paperwork in order for this program.

9. **Children's College Savings**
   - ☐ Review *Chapters 9 and 10.*
   - ☐ Don't try to cash flow your children's college expenses, save up for them.
   - ☐ Visit savingforcollege.org and calculate what you need to save.

10. Retirement Savings

- ☐ Calculate how much you would like to have when you retire.
- ☐ Maximize your group's retirement vehicles, then branch out on your own.
- ☐ Do not neglect your own retirement savings for your children's college.

11. Your Education Fund

- ☐ Learn how to maximize your education/travel fund.

12. Brief Asset Protection

a. Protect

- ☐ Your Career with Medical Malpractice
- ☐ Your Income with Life and Disability Insurance.
- ☐ Your Marriage by spending time with your spouse and time on your marriage.
- ☐ Your Home - buy a home you can afford.
- ☐ Your investments:
    1. Learn how to invest money on your own.
    2. If you don't have the time/inclination, then hire a fee only CFP.

Chapter 35
Bonus Chapter: Part-Time Work and Job Sharing

Some physicians would like to cut back on working hours to spend more time with family, travel, or enjoy life more.

Some specialties are more amenable to part time work and can job share.

1. **Before Deciding to do Part Time Work / Job Sharing**
    a. Understand that it can change the dynamics of:
        i. Your relationships within your practice group.
            1. Even though you are getting paid less (see below), some people may resent that you are working less than they are.
            2. You might not get a full say in the decisions of the group.
        ii. Your stability within your practice group:
            1. Because you are not working full time, your job may be less needed or at higher risk for non-renewal of your contract.
            2. If you start working part time, they could reduce your hours further, if work slows down.
            3. It could also limit the leadership roles you could potentially have in the department.

2. **Park-Time Work**
    a. There are various amounts of time that would be considered "part time" work for a physician.
        i. This may be 80% (working 4 days/week) to 20% (working 1 day/week).
        ii. This may also mean taking less call or no call.
    b. Part-Time Work does not equal Part Time Money:
        i. 80% work will not automatically equal 80% salary.
            1. There are certain fixed costs associated with your job.
                a. Medical malpractice insurance
                b. Office personnel
                c. Billing personnel
                d. Your health insurance
                e. Your retirement/benefit management
                    i. Most benefit packages cost your employer about 30% of your salary.
                    ii. For Example: A physician earning $200k actually costs their employer $260k including retirement/benefits.
        ii. You may also accrue vacation and sick leave at a different rate, compared to your colleagues that are working full time.
        iii. Once you go part time, you will be accruing retirement savings at a lower rate as well, which may postpone your time till you are able to retire.

3. **Part Time Contract Work**
   a. As a contract employee, you won't have as much representation in the group.
      i. However, it can potentially give you more flexibility compared to full time physicians.
   b. It is best if you can get medical malpractice through the group you are contracting with.
      i. You can potentially get a better rate.
      ii. It is very difficult to get a price break on medical malpractice insurance working part-time unless you are working very few hours.
         1. Then working part-time would probably not be worth it.
      iii. If you do buy your own, try and get the tail coverage rolled into the premium, if your only working for a short period of time for the employer.

4. **Job Sharing**
   a. Typically, this is when two physicians share the same job or Full Time Equivalent (FTE).
      i. Call duties, work load, and possibly vacation are also shared.
   b. Job Sharing can be a viable alternative to those looking for part time work in a group that only has full time work arrangements.
   c. If this arrangement is made, clear guidelines need to be written out.
      i. Expectations and responsibilities must be clearly defined.
   d. Much like part time work, job sharing will also not pay exactly half of the salary, because your group will be providing twice the number of benefits for one FTE.
   e. There is also the risk that you may have to work full time again, if the other person sharing the FTE leaves that position.

Chapter 36
Epilogue

I hope you have enjoyed this book.

If you have any comments, corrections, or suggestions for future topics to be included within the next edition, please send me an e-mail at Physician.Feedback@ProFinanceGuides.com

Also, please take the time to rate this book on Amazon. I really appreciate your feedback.

Many Thanks:
Steiny

38608835R00060

Made in the USA
Lexington, KY
17 January 2015